3

College Oral
Communication

3

College Oral Communication

ENGLISH FOR ACADEMIC SUCCESS

Cheryl L. Delk
Georgia State University

SERIES EDITORS

Patricia Byrd

Joy M. Reid

Cynthia M. Schuemann

THOMSON

™

HEINLE

Australia • Canada • Mexico • Singapore • Spain • United Kingdom • United States

College Oral Communication 3
English for Academic Success
Cheryl L. Delk

Publisher: Patricia A. Coryell
Director of ESL Publishing: Susan Maguire
Senior Development Editor: Kathy Sands Boehmer
Editorial Assistant: Evangeline Bermas

Senior Project Editor: Kathryn Dinovo
Manufacturing Assistant: Karmen Chong
Senior Marketing Manager: Annamarie Rice

Printed in the United States of America.
2 3 4 5 6 7 8 9 10   09 08 07

For more information contact Thomson Heinle, 25 Thomson Place, Boston, MA 02210 USA, or visit our Internet site at elt.thomson.com

Library of Congress Control Number: 2004112190

ISBN 10: 0-618-23018-1
ISBN 13: 978-0-618-23018-1

Cover graphics: © LMA Communications, Natick, Massachusetts

Photo credits: © Larry Lee/Corbis, p. 1; © Bettmann/Corbis, p. 7; © Paris Claude/Corbis Sygma p. 7; ThinkQuest, p. 26; Getty Images, p. 30; Getty Images, p. 40; © Steve Prezant/Corbis, p. 53; © Royalty-Free/Corbis, p. 53; © Image 100/Royalty-Free/Corbis, p. 53; © Jose Luis Pelaez, Inc./Corbis, p. 54; © Bettmann/Corbis, p. 54; © Royalty-Free/Corbis, p. 54; © Jose Luis Pelaez, Inc./Corbis, p. 81; id software, p. 110; © Joseph Sohm; ChromoSohm Inc./Corbis, p. 142; *Albany Times Union*, p. 151; © Reuters/Corbis, p. 159

Text credits: Excerpt from "Computer Animation and the Cinema World," by Mahmooda Sultana, from Illumin. Reprinted by permission. For more information: http://illumin.usc.edu, p. 30; Source: http://www.nielsenmedia.com. Reprinted by permission of Nielsen Media Research, p. 84; Source: Television Bureau of Advertising (TVB) from estimates supplied by TNS Media Intelligence/CMR, p. 86; Source: MAGNA Global USA analysis of copyrighted Nielsen Media Research data. Reprinted by permission of Nielsen Media Research and with permission from Jack Myers Report. p. 87; Reprinted by permission of the Newspaper Association of America Foundation, p. 103; Source: Slightly adapted from http://www.nielsenmedia.com. Reprinted by permission of Nielsen Media Research, p.105; Adapted activity from "The Violence Formula: Analyzing TV, Video, and Movies" by Barbara Osborn, from www.medialit.org/reading_room/article94.html. Reprinted by permission of the Center for Media Literacy, p. 137; Frommer, Frederic J., "Group Cites Video-Game Makers for Violence Against Women," Associated Press, December 19, 2002. Reprinted with permission of The Associated Press, p. 116; From Society of Professional Journalists, 3909 N. Meridian St., Indianapolis, Indiana 46208, www.spj.org. Copyright © 2004 by Society of Professional Journalists. Reprinted by permission, p. 147; Excerpted from Newskit: A Consumers Guide to News Media by Jeffrey Schrank, The Learning Seed Co. Used by permission of the author, p. 153; Selected Case Studies #1 and #9, (slightly adapted to include questions) from "You Were the Editor" by Gary Wisby, *Chicago Sun-Times*, Sunday, July 23, 2000. Reprinted with special permission from the Chicago Sun-Times, Inc., © 2004 and 2000, p. 157; Selected Case Studies #2, "Editorial POVs," and #5, "Story," (slightly adapted to include questions), London (Ontario) Free Press. Reprinted by permission, p. 157

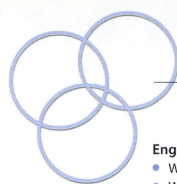

Contents

English for Academic Success Series

CHAPTER 1

How Did Movies Get Started?

ACADEMIC FOCUS: HUMANITIES ▶ FILM HISTORY   1

CHAPTER 2

How'd They Do That?

ACADEMIC FOCUS: COMPUTER SCIENCE ▶ COMPUTER ANIMATION TECHNOLOGY   26

CHAPTER 3

Can You Hear Me Now?

ACADEMIC FOCUS: SOCIAL SCIENCE ▶ COMMUNICATION STUDIES   53

English for Academic Success Series

SERIES EDITORS

Patricia Byrd, Joy M. Reid, Cynthia M. Schuemann

○ What Is the Purpose of This Series?

The English for Academic Success series is a comprehensive program of student and instructor materials: four levels of student language proficiency textbooks in three skill areas (oral communication, reading, and writing), with supplemental vocabulary textbooks at each level. For instructors and students, a useful website supports classroom teaching, learning, and assessment. For instructors, four Essentials of Teaching Academic Language books, (*Essentials of Teaching Academic Oral Communication*, *Essentials of Teaching Academic Reading*, *Essentials of Teaching Academic Writing*, and *Essentials of Teaching Academic Vocabulary*) provide helpful information for instructors new to teaching oral communication, reading, writing, and vocabulary.

The fundamental purpose of the series is to prepare students who are not native speakers of English for academic success in U.S. college degree programs. By studying these materials, students in college English-for-Academic-Purposes (EAP) courses will gain the academic language skills they need to be successful students in degree programs. Additionally, students will learn about being successful students in U.S. college courses.

The series is based on considerable prior research as well as our own investigations of students' needs and interests, instructors' needs and desires, and institutional expectations and requirements. For example, our survey research revealed what problems instructors feel they face in their classrooms and what they actually teach; who the students are and what they know and do not know about the "culture" of U.S. colleges; and what types of exams are required for admission at various colleges.

Student Audience

The materials in this series are for college-bound ESL students at U.S. community colleges and undergraduate programs at other institutions. Some of these students are U.S. high school graduates. Some of them are long-term U.S. residents who graduated from a high school before coming to the United States. Others are newer U.S. residents. Still others are more typical international students. All of them need to develop academic language skills and knowledge of ways to be successful in U.S. college degree courses.

All of the books in this series have been created to implement the English for Academic Success competencies. These competencies are based on those developed by ESL instructors and administrators in Florida, California, and Connecticut to be the underlying structure for EAP courses at colleges in those states. These widely respected competencies assure that the materials meet the real world needs of EAP students and instructors.

All of the books focus on . . .

- Starting where the students are, building on their strengths and prior knowledge (which is considerable, if not always academically relevant), and helping students self-identify needs and plans to strengthen academic language skills
- Academic English, including development of Academic Vocabulary and grammar required by students for academic speaking/listening, reading, and writing
- Master Student Skills, including learning style analysis, strategy training, and learning about the "culture" of U.S. colleges, which lead to their becoming successful students in degree courses and degree programs
- Topics and readings that represent a variety of academic disciplinary areas so that students learn about the language and content of the social sciences, the hard sciences, education, and business as well as the humanities
- Interesting and valuable content that helps the students develop their knowledge of academic content as well as their language skills and student skills
- A wide variety of practical classroom-tested activities that are easy to teach and engage the students

- Assessment tools at the end of each chapter so that instructors have easy-to-implement ways to assess student learning and students have opportunities to assess their own growth
- Websites for the students and for the instructors: the student sites will provide additional opportunities to practice reading, writing, listening, vocabulary development, and grammar. The instructor sites will provide instructor's manuals, teaching notes and answer keys, value-added materials like handouts and overheads that can be reproduced to use in class, and assessment tools such as additional tests to use beyond the assessment materials in each book.

○ What Is the Purpose of the Oral Communication Strand?

The Oral Communication strand of English for Academic Success focuses on development of speaking and listening skills necessary for college study. Dedicated to meeting academic needs of students by teaching them how to handle the spoken English used by instructors and students in college classrooms, the four books provide engaging activities to practice both academic listening and academic speaking. Students learn to participate effectively in a variety of academic situations, including discussions, lectures, student study groups, and office meetings with their college instructors.

Because of the importance of academic vocabulary in the spoken English of the classroom, the oral communication strand teaches the students techniques for learning and using new academic vocabulary both to recognize the words when they hear them and to use the words in their own spoken English. Grammar appropriate to the listening and speaking activities is also included in each chapter. For example, Book 2 includes work with the pronunciation of irregular past tense verbs as part of learning how to listen to and participate in academic discussions focused on history. In addition to language development, the books provide for academic skill development through the teaching of appropriate academic tasks and the giving of master student tips to help students better understand what is expected of them in college classes. Students learn to carry out academic tasks in ways that are linguistically, academically, and culturally appropriate. For example, students learn how to take information from the spoken presentations by their instructors and then to use that information for other academic tasks such as tests or small group discussions. That is, students are not taught to take notes for some abstract reason but learn to make a powerful connection between note-taking and success in other assigned tasks.

Each book has a broad disciplinary theme to give coherence to the content. These themes were selected because of their high interest for students; they are also topics commonly explored in introductory college courses and so provide useful background for students. Materials were selected that are academically appropriate but that do not require expert knowledge by the instructor. The following themes are used: Book 1: Human Psychology, Book 2: The Connections between Human Beings and Animals, Book 3: Communication and Media, and Book 4: Money. For example, Book 1 has one chapter about the psychological effects of music and another on the relationship between nutrition and psychological well-being. Book 2 uses topics such as taboo foods, animals as workers, using animals in medical and scientific testing, along with one of Aesop's fables. Book 3 includes the history of movies, computer animation, privacy rights, and other topics related to modern media. Book 4 takes on a topic that fascinates most students with various themes related to money, including such related topics as the history of money, marketing use of psychological conditioning, and the economics of the World Wide Web. These topics provide high-interest content for use in the listening and speaking activities, but do not require that instructors have to develop any new knowledge to be able to use the materials.

Instructor Support Materials

Recorded materials presented in each chapter are available on an audiotape or CD that is provided with each book. In addition to a recording of the main lecture for each chapter, the recording includes other materials such as dialogues and academic vocabulary.

The series also includes a resource book for instructors called *Essentials of Teaching Academic Oral Communication* by John Murphy. This practical book provides strategies and activities for the use of instructors new to the teaching of oral communication.

○ What Is the Organization of *College Oral Communication 3*?

College Oral Communication 3 prepares high-intermediate level students for the demands of college-level academic listening and speaking tasks. Six chapters of readings and lectures in history, technology, communication, business, sociology, and ethics present concepts and language that many students will encounter in future college courses.

Vocabulary is a prominent feature of the textbook. Each chapter provides a list of academic words related to the reading and lecture, supported by pronunciation work in syllable number and stress.

Master Student Tips scattered throughout the textbook provide students with short comments on a particular strategy, activity, or practical advice to follow in an academic setting.

Chapter Organization

Each chapter is clearly divided into three sections: Effective Academic Listening, Effective Academic Speaking, and Assessing Your Listening and Speaking Skills.

Effective Academic Listening

Getting Ready for the Lecture Readings, charts and tables engage students in the content and prepare them to listen and take notes from lectures. Note-taking strategies such as recognizing signal words for different patterns of organization, using symbols and abbreviations, and working with content vocabulary prepare students to listen and take notes from academic lectures and classroom communication.

Getting Information from the Lecture Students are guided toward successful note-taking by predicting content and organization. Students listen to academic lectures and use provided outlines as models of effective note-taking.

Making Your Notes Useful Students participate in academic tasks directly related to their notes and the content of the particular chapter. Tasks include preparing an oral summary, predicting test questions, making study aids such as graphic organizers or concept cards, processing notes with a recall column, and using notes to synthesize lecture and reading content.

Effective Academic Speaking

Activities in this section all resemble types of academic tasks expected of students in the college environment such as taking on roles and participating in small group formal and informal discussions on lecture content, case studies, or personal experiences, presenting oral summaries, giving short presentations, providing feedback to classmates' presentations, giving a short presentation and providing feedback to a classmate, and leaving effective voicemail messages.

Assessing Your Listening and Speaking Skills

Additional academic listening and speaking and note-taking tasks are provided with similar content material to allow students to demonstrate that they have mastered the objectives of the chapter. In addition, students are given the opportunity to reflect on several of the academic strategies they learned and practiced in the chapter. Each chapter ends with a listing of the chapter objectives for students to evaluate their progress.

Acknowledgments

The energy and enthusiasm that it takes to write a textbook comes from many different sources. The ESL developmental editor, Kathy Sands Boehmer, was encouraging and patient as we bombarded her with multiple questions on multiple occasions. The series editors Patricia Byrd, Joy Reid, and Cynthia Schuemann, along with fellow Oral Communication authors Marsha Chan, Ann Roemer, and Steve Jones shared their experience, knowledge, and never-ending words of support during countless individual and group e-mail exchanges and conference calls.

I am particularly grateful for one of my advisors, Mary Lu Light, a close friend and former colleague, who consistently asked "How's the book going?" and patiently listened and advised me on my thought processes. My other advisors, Anne Bruehler and Rose Camelo, also provided useful feedback and an important perspective to early drafts.

The following reviewers contributed practical comments for the entire book and specific activities:

Marsha Abramovich, Tidewater Community College
Darenda Borgers, Broward Community College
William Brazda, Long Beach City College
Charlotte Calobrisi, Northern Virginia Community College
Linda Choi, Canada College
Elaine Dow, Quinsagamond Community College
Mark Ende, Onondaga Community College
Margo Harder, South Seattle Community College
Shirley Terrell, Collin County Community College
Amy Tickle, Minneapolis, MN
Denise Teicher, Norwalk Community College
Hoda Zaki, Camden County College
Kathy Zuo, William Rainey Harper College

And I am indebted to the family members, friends, and former and current colleagues who helped pull me through this process, offering real-time encouragement and support when needed most.

Finally, I thank the students. I am inspired by the ones I have watched take countless risks and sacrifice much to meet their goals and left me with the desire to do the same.

⭕ What Student Competencies Are Covered in *College Oral Communication 3*?

English for Academic Success Competencies *College Oral Communication 3*

Description of Overall Purposes

Students develop communication, organization, and pronunciation skills necessary for effective academic presentation and discussion with an introduction to lecture note taking.

With the Materials in This Book, a Student Will Learn:

Production

Competency 1: The student will speak with sufficient accuracy and fluency to ensure comprehension in many professional and academic situations. The student will have a few strategies for helping others to understand her/him.

Competency 2: The student will speak with intelligible pronunciation, stress and intonation.

Competency 3: The student will demonstrate the ability to deliver presentations in classroom settings and explain and support opinions.

Competency 4: The student will speak extemporaneously on diverse topics.

Comprehension

Competency 5: The student will paraphrase basic information or opinions from original sources and credit the source.

Competency 6: The student will take notes during instructor lectures and student presentations and summarize the content. The student will use notes for academic tasks such as preparing for examinations.

Competency 7: The student will edit and correct his/her own spoken English while participating in academic tasks such as classroom presentations or small group discussions.

Competency 8: The student will adjust his/her listening strategies to the task at hand.

Competency 9: The student will demonstrate analytical listening skills:
   a. Distinguish facts from generalizations/theory.
   b. Make inferences.
   c. Identify speaker's purpose, point of view, and tone.
   d. Comprehend use of figurative language.

◯ What Are the Features of the Oral Communication Books?

The English for Academic Success series is a comprehensive program of student and instructor materials. The fundamental purpose of the program is to prepare students who are not native speakers of English for academic success in U.S. college degree programs.

The Oral Communication strand of the English for Academic Success series focuses on development of speaking and listening skills necessary for college study. Dedicated to meeting academic needs of students by teaching them how to handle the spoken English used by instructors and students in college classrooms, the four books provide engaging activities to practice both academic listening and academic speaking. Students learn to participate effectively in a variety of academic situations, including discussions, lectures, study groups, and office meetings with their college instructors.

Broad Disciplinary Themes: Each book has a broad disciplinary theme to give coherence to the content. These themes were selected because of their high interest for students. They are also topics commonly explored in introductory college courses and so provide useful background for students.

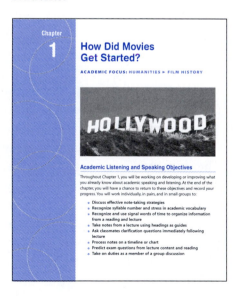

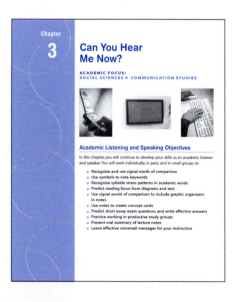

Effective Academic Listening: Students listen to authentic classroom interactions and lectures. They learn to take information from the spoken presentations and use their notes for other academic tasks such as tests or small group discussions.

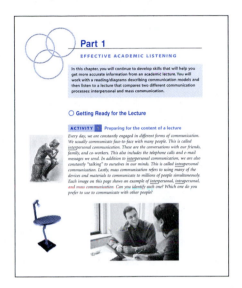

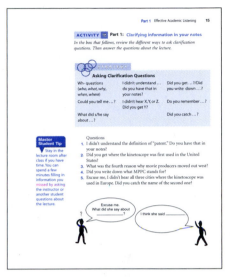

Effective Academic Speaking: Speaking tasks resemble types of academic tasks expected of students in the college environment. These speaking tasks include taking on roles and participating in small group formal and informal discussions on lecture content, presenting oral summaries, to leaving effective voicemail messages. Students learn to do oral presentations appropriate to their proficiency level and to college study.

Self-Assessment of Academic Listening and Speaking Skills: Students are given the opportunity to reflect on several of the academic strategies they learned and practiced in the chapters. Each chapter ends with a listing of the chapter objectives for students to evaluate their progress.

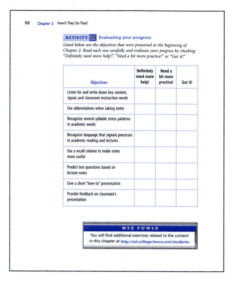

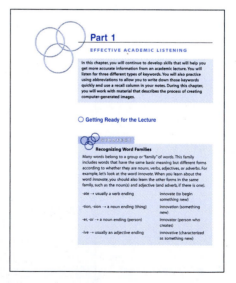

Academic Vocabulary: The Oral Communication strand teaches students techniques for learning and using new academic vocabulary in order to recognize the words when they hear them and to also use the words in their own spoken English.

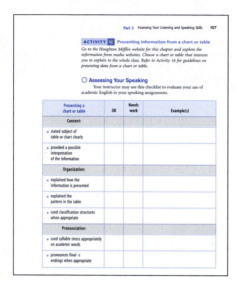

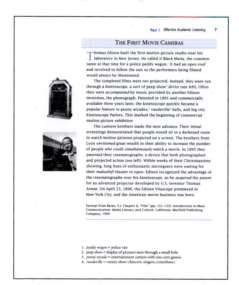

Academic Listening and Speaking Strategies: Key strategies and skills are interspersed throughout each book. Students can clearly see important concepts to focus on as they complete the activities in each chapter. Highlighted strategies will help students improve both their listening and speaking skills.

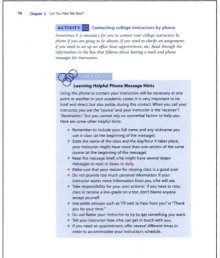

Master Student Tips: Master Student Tips throughout the textbooks provide students with short comments on a particular strategy, activity, or practical advice to follow in an academic setting. Instructors can use these tips to help students become better students by building their understanding of college study.

Power Grammar Boxes: Students can be very diverse in their grammar and rhetorical needs so each chapter contains Power Grammar boxes that introduce the grammar structures students need to be fluent and accurate in academic English.

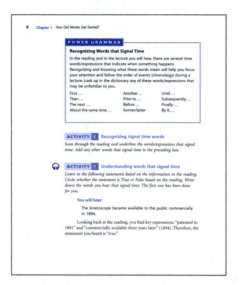

Ancillary Program: The following items are available to accompany the English for Academic Success series Oral Communication strand.

- Instructor website: Additional teaching materials, activities, and robust student assessment.
- Student website: Additional exercises and activities.
- Audio Program: Available on either CD-ROM or cassette.
- The English for Academic Success series Vocabulary books: You can choose the appropriate level to shrinkwrap with your text.
- *Essentials of Teaching Academic Oral Communication* by John Murphy is available for purchase. It gives you theoretical and practical information for teaching oral communication.

How Did Movies Get Started?

ACADEMIC FOCUS: HUMANITIES ▶ FILM HISTORY

Academic Listening and Speaking Objectives

Throughout Chapter 1, you will be working on developing or improving what you already know about academic speaking and listening. At the end of the chapter, you will have a chance to return to these objectives and record your progress. You will work individually, in pairs, and in small groups to:

- Discuss effective note-taking strategies
- Recognize syllable number and stress in academic vocabulary
- Recognize and use signal words of time to organize information from a reading and lecture
- Take notes from a lecture using headings as guides
- Ask classmates clarification questions immediately following lecture
- Process notes on a timeline or chart
- Predict exam questions from lecture content and reading
- Take on duties as a member of a group discussion

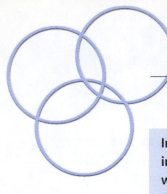

Part 1

EFFECTIVE ACADEMIC LISTENING

In this chapter, you will practice skills that will help you obtain accurate information from an academic lecture in the form of lecture notes. You will learn how to use this information to make graphic organizers and predict questions for a test. During this chapter, you will be working with material that describes the history of making movies.

○ Getting Ready for the Lecture

Throughout this book, you are going to take notes from lectures. Let's start by thinking about and discussing why students take notes during lectures.

ACTIVITY 1 Reflecting on note-taking

Take a few minutes to write down your opinions about these questions.

1. In your opinion, why is it necessary to take notes during lectures?
2. What do you do to help yourself take better notes? In other words, do you have any personal "tricks" such as abbreviating words, using certain symbols, making charts, etc.?

ACTIVITY 2 Comparing your notes with a classmate

Sit with one of your classmates, and compare your answers to the questions in the previous activity. Combine the information from both of your answers in the space provided, and discuss any similarities and/or differences.

Reasons to take notes	Personal "tricks"	Ways to improve

ACTIVITY **3** **Analyzing effective note-taking strategies**

In small groups, look at the following chart of effective note-taking strategies. Discuss why using each of these strategies could help you become a better note-taker. Write down all of your group's ideas on the chart.

Suggested note-taking strategies	Reasons why these strategies could be helpful
Include name, date, and lecture topic at top of page	*to be able to remember several weeks later; to borrow and lend out notes easily*
Sit near the instructor	
Read related textbook material before lecture	
Record all important words	
Separate general ideas from specific ideas ● by indenting examples ● by indenting details	
Leave white space in your notes	
Use abbreviations and symbols	
Do not sit near the door, window, or talkative students	
Do not try to write every word	
Revise your notes soon after class to make them clearer	

Master Student Tip

During whole-class discussions, it's important not to "tune out." Pay attention to what your classmates say; they may have ideas that you did not think about. You should include these ideas in your notes.

ACTIVITY 4   Filling in missing information

Your instructor will facilitate the whole class in compiling the information from Activity 3. Fill in any new information in the note-taking strategy chart that you may have missed.

ACTIVITY 5   Using context to learn word meanings

The words that follow are found in the first reading and in the lecture you will hear. Use context (how the words are used) to figure out the meanings of the underlined words. Choose the correct definition from the list (there is one extra definition).

a. to imagine; foresee
b. made using whatever is available
c. provided together with something else
d. at the beginning
e. at the same time
f. at the end
g. made bright with light
h. developments
i. to obtain something
j. machine invented for a certain use
k. right to make and sell something

1. _____ Many <u>advances</u> have been made in cancer research.

2. _____ Since we didn't have much money, we made <u>makeshift</u> tables for our apartment with boxes and wooden crates.

3. _____ I asked the waiter if a salad would <u>accompany</u> my steak.

4. _____ An inventor usually gets a <u>patent</u> for a new invention before it is mass produced and sold in stores.

5. _____ You must <u>acquire</u> permission to sign up for that course directly from the professor.

6. _____ Successful inventors are often able to <u>envision</u> how our lives will be easier with certain products.

7. _____ The early <u>devices</u> used to take photos were much larger than the mini-cameras you can find today.

8. _____ In order to meet people, you often have to take the <u>initial</u> step and introduce yourself rather than wait for people to talk to you first.

9. _____ The night sky was <u>illuminated</u> with lights from the city.

10. _____ I can only concentrate on one thing, so it is impossible for me to <u>simultaneously</u> watch TV and do my homework.

STRATEGY

Learning the Stress Patterns of New Words

This book uses a numbering system to identify the number of syllables and the strongest syllable in words to help you learn how to analyze and pronounce new words. In each English word, there is one syllable that is the longest, loudest, and highest in pitch. Recognizing that syllable, both in speaking and in listening, is important for effective communication.

Here's an example. Listen to your instructor pronounce the word "device":

de • vice´

We can see that this word has two syllables and the stress is on the second syllable. Tap your fingers twice on the table as you say "device." Tap and pronounce the word again, putting extra stress on the second syllable.

An easy way to remember how to pronounce this word is to write the number of syllables, and then the number of the stressed syllable, with a dash [-] between the two numbers. For example, for "device" write "2-2," meaning that the word has two syllables and the second syllable is stressed.

Listen to your instructor pronounce the word "illuminate":

il • lu´• mi • nate

Tap your fingers four times on the table as you hear the word. Tap and pronounce the word, putting stress on the second syllable. We can identify this word as a "4-2 word."

ACTIVITY 6   **Learning the pronunciation of new words**

Listen to the pronunciation of these words. Use the numbering system to indicate how many syllables are in each word and which syllable is stressed. Then, practice pronouncing these words out loud with a partner.

1. patent   [_2_ - _1_]

2. accompany   [___ - ___]   *pro***JEC***tor [3-2]*

3. advance   [___ - ___]

4. initial   [___ - ___]   *exhi***BI***tion [4-3]*

5. envision   [___ - ___]

6. simultaneous   [___ - ___]   **PHO***tograph [3-1]*

7. makeshift   [___ - ___]

8. acquire   [___ - ___]

STRATEGY

Academic Word List

In this textbook, you will learn vocabulary that occurs in college-level, or academic, situations. This vocabulary is from a list called the Academic Word List (AWL). The AWL is a set of words that have been found in examples of writing in many different college subjects. Learning the AWL words will help you to understand lectures or readings in many different college classes.

Master Student Tip

Reading related material before listening to the lecture can help you recognize unfamiliar words and names when you hear them for the first time.

ACTIVITY 7   **Reading material to prepare for the lecture**

Read the following textbook excerpt to prepare for the lecture on the history of film production. The vocabulary words from the preceding activity are italicized.

THE FIRST MOVIE CAMERAS

Thomas Edison built the first motion picture studio near his laboratory in New Jersey. He called it Black Maria, the common name at that time for a police paddy wagon.[1] It had an open roof and revolved to follow the sun so the performers being filmed would always be illuminated.

The completed films were not projected. Instead, they were run through a kinetoscope, a sort of peep show[2] *device* (see left). Often they were *accompanied* by music provided by another Edison invention, the phonograph. Patented in 1891 and commercially available three years later, the kinetoscope quickly became a popular feature in penny arcades,[3] vaudeville[4] halls, and big city Kinetoscope Parlors. This marked the beginning of commercial motion picture *exhibition*.

The Lumiere brothers made the next *advance*. Their *initial* screenings demonstrated that people would sit in a darkened room to watch motion pictures projected on a screen. The brothers from Lyon *envisioned* great wealth in their ability to increase the number of people who could *simultaneously* watch a movie. In 1895 they *patented* their cinematographe, a device that both photographed and projected action (see left). Within weeks of their Christmastime showing, long lines of enthusiastic moviegoers were waiting for their *makeshift* theater to open. Edison recognized the advantage of the cinematographe over his kinetoscope, so he *acquired* the *patent* for an advanced projector developed by U.S. inventor Thomas Armat. On April 23, 1896, the Edison Vitascope premiered in New York City, and the American movie business was born.

Excerpt from Baran, S.J. Chapter 6, "Film" (pp. 151–152). Introduction to Mass Communication: Media Literacy and Culture. California: Mayfield Publishing Company, 1999

1. *paddy wagon* = police van
2. *peep show* = display of pictures seen through a small hole
3. *penny arcade* = entertainment centers with one-cent games
4. *vaudeville* = variety show (dancers, singers, comedians)

POWER GRAMMAR

Recognizing Words that Signal Time

In the reading and in the lecture you will hear, there are several time words/expressions that indicate when something happens. Recognizing and knowing what these words mean will help you focus your attention and follow the order of events (chronology) during a lecture. Look up in the dictionary any of these words/expressions that may be unfamiliar to you.

First . . .	Another . . .	Until . . .
Then . . .	Prior to . . .	Subsequently . . .
The next . . .	Before . . .	Finally . . .
About the same time . . .	former/latter	By X, . . .
_____	_____	_____

ACTIVITY 8 **Recognizing signal time words**

Scan through the reading and underline the words/expressions that signal time. Add any other words that signal time to the preceding box.

 ACTIVITY 9 **Understanding words that signal time**

Listen to the following statements based on the information in the reading. Circle whether the statement is True or False based on the reading. Write down the words you hear that signal time. The first one has been done for you.

You will hear:

> The kinetoscope became available to the public commercially in 1894.

Looking back at the reading, you find key expressions: "patented in 1891" and "commercially available three years later" (1894). Therefore, the statement you heard is "*true.*"

                        Signal Words

1. (True) / False   *In 1894*

2. True / False

3. True / False

4. True / False

5. True / False

6. True / False

◯ Getting Information from the Lecture

    Successful students have strategies for predicting what a lecture is going to be about. Students don't write down all of these strategies. Some are things they think about—mental processes such as predicting what the instructor will say and figuring out the organization of the lecture in advance.

ACTIVITY 10   **Predicting what your instructor will say**

Based on the reading and what you already might know about movie history, write down your predictions of key names and words/ideas you think you will hear in the lecture. Work with a partner to combine your lists into an expanded list. A few examples are provided for you.

Names/People	Words/Ideas
Edison	patent

ACTIVITY **11** Listening for the organization in the lecture

Listen to the introduction of the lecture, and write down a few words/phrases of what you think each of the lecture's three sections will be about. Also, write down the signal words the instructor used to distinguish the different sections. Part 1 is done as an example.

	Main idea of section	**Words that signal time**
Part 1	inventor/inventions	to start end of 19th century
Part 2		
Part 3		

 ACTIVITY **12** **Part 1:** Taking notes from the lecture

This time, listen to the entire first section of the lecture. Follow along with these notes. Discuss the questions at the end with the whole class.

History of Movie Production

- Inventions and Inventors
  - Thomas Edison–American inventor
    - Invented electric lamp & phonograph
    - Patented over 1,000 inventions
      - "Patent" ≠ "invent" (patent = owning the rights to make or sell invention)
    - Worked with British inventor William Dickson

Kinetograph & Kinetoscope

To record movement   To view films

◆ Kinetoscope patented in 1891
  ● First used 4/14/1894 in NYC
  ● Used in London, Berlin, & Paris (same year)
  ● Only one person/kinetoscope (Edison thought he could make the most $$ this way)
■ Other inventors/inventions
  ▲ Lumiere brothers (Auguste & Louis) in France
    ◆ First projector-cinematographe-in 1895
      ● Diff. from kinetoscope b/c many people could watch a movie at the same time
    ◆ Filmmakers
      ● One of 1st films-train coming into station
        ★ People were scared-not used to moving pictures (audience involvement)
■ Edison's desire to keep up with competition
  ▲ 1896-patented rights to a projector inv. by Thomas Armat
  ▲ Renamed it "Edison Vitascope"
  ▲ To make money and control movies

Questions to consider

1. What strategies are used in the preceding notes that make them easy to follow?
2. How can you tell the difference between a main idea and a detail/example in these notes?
3. What strategies from these notes do you think you might try in your own notes?

Part 2: **Taking notes to get information from the lecture**

This time, listen to the rest of the lecture. Use the main headings to guide you.

Master Student Tip

Using indentation and markers such as ●, ■, and ▲, are helpful and sometimes easier to use than numbering and lettering systems (I, II, A, a., etc.).

● Monopolization of the film industry–beginning of 20ᵗʰ century
    ■ Formation of MPPC

    ■ MPPC rules

● Effects of monopoly on movie industry
    ■ Reasons independents fled to CA

    ■ Other reasons for move out west

    ■ Other important events in Hollywood in early 20ᵗʰ century

ACTIVITY 13 Confirming your predictions

Go back to your list of predictions in Activity 10. Circle the words that you and your classmates predicted would be in the lecture that the instructor mentioned. Confirm the spelling of these words with your classmates or your instructor and make any adjustments in your notes.

◯ Making Your Notes Useful

Sometimes students realize that their notes are not complete because they didn't understand/hear what the instructor said or because they just didn't have time to write everything down. Successful students take time immediately after a lecture to be sure that their notes are as complete as possible. They look back at the textbook material, or they ask classmates or the instructor specific questions about their notes.

ACTIVITY 14 Making a graphic organizer

You can use your information from your notes to make study guides to help organize and remember the information from a lecture. A timeline is a good study guide to use with notes from lectures that are based on historical topics. Look at the examples of different timelines.

Horizontal Timeline

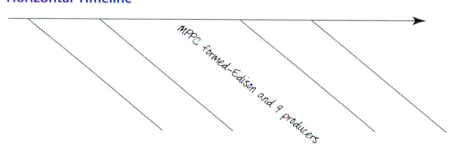

MPPC formed–Edison and 9 producers

Vertical Timeline

1908	MPPC was formed by Edison and 9 other producers

A chart usually gives you more space to fill in important information. Fill in the chart that follows with the appropriate information from your lecture notes.

Time	Important events	Significant people
1891		
1894		
1895		
1896		
1908	MPPC was formed	Edison and 9 other producers
1911		--------------------
1912		--------------------
1915		

ACTIVITY 15 Part 1: Clarifying information in your notes

In the box that follows, review the different ways to ask clarification questions. Then answer the questions about the lecture.

STRATEGY

Asking Clarification Questions

Wh- questions (*who, what, why, when, where*)	I didn't understand … do you have that in your notes?	Did you get …?/Did you write down …?
Could you tell me …?	I didn't hear X, Y, or Z. Did you get Y?	Do you remember …?
What did s/he say about …?		Did you catch …?

Questions

1. I didn't understand the definition of "patent." Do you have that in your notes?
2. Did you get where the kinetoscope was first used in the United States?
3. What was the fourth reason why movie producers moved out west?
4. Did you write down what MPPC stands for?
5. Excuse me, I didn't hear all three cities where the kinetoscope was used in Europe. Did you catch the name of the second one?

Part 2: Asking questions to clarify information in your notes

Create five questions of your own based on information in your notes that may be unclear or that you have questions about. Write your questions in the space below. Share your questions with your classmates and prepare to answer their questions.

1. _____

_____

2. _____

_____

3. _____

_____

4. _____

_____

5. _____

_____

ACTIVITY 16   Summarizing parts of the lecture

Take turns retelling the parts of the lecture to a partner. When you are the speaker, use your timeline/chart to remind you of the content. When you are the listener, help the speaker with keywords or ideas.

Example: In 1908, the MPPC was formed when Edison and nine other movie producers got together to try to control the movie industry. It was similar to the business people who wanted to control other industries such as oil or the railroad.

Student A: 1891
1895
1911
1915

Student B: 1894
1896
1912

ACTIVITY 17 Predicting short answer exam questions

You can do better on tests if you prepare for questions by predicting what some of them will be from the lecture and reading. You can learn the answers in advance and be better prepared. Use question words such as why, when, who, what, where, *and* how *to predict questions based on your notes and timeline chart. For homework, write the answers to these questions in the space provided.*

Why, When, Who, What, Where, How Questions

1. **Question:** Who developed the first projector that could be used by many spectators at the same time?

   Answer: The Lumiere Brothers

2. **Question:** _____

   Answer: _____

3. **Question:** _____

   Answer: _____

Part 2

EFFECTIVE ACADEMIC SPEAKING

Sometimes after a lecture an instructor might put students into smaller groups so they can discuss lecture content and the outside reading. Another reason that instructors might use groups is so that students can get to know each other better to discuss topics related to the lecture. In this section, you are going to be involved in group discussions to practice participating more effectively.

ACTIVITY 18 Expressing agreement and disagreement

Read the following lists of possible expressions you can use to agree and disagree with your peers. Add other expressions that you might use.

S T R A T E G Y

Expressing Agreement and Disagreement

Disagreement	Agreement
I disagree because …	That's true.
But don't you think …	I agree with what X said.
That may be true, but …	I think so too.
I see your point, but …	Yeah, that's what I think too.
Well, I wouldn't necessarily agree with …	I don't think so either.
Yes, but I think …	You might/may/could be right.
But you have to remember …	That makes sense.
Do you really think so? I thought …	Exactly! I couldn't agree more.
But the reading says …	Yes, in the lecture, s/he said …
_____	_____
_____	_____

ACTIVITY 19 Using terms of agreement and disagreement

Read the statements that follow. Add the necessary words to one of the expressions from Activity 18 to write a more polite response that expresses disagreement.

1. **A:** All violence should be eliminated from movies to protect children.
    B: That doesn't make sense at all.
More polite response:

_____

2. **A:** Tom Hanks is the worst actor I've ever seen.
    B: You're crazy to think that.
More polite response:

_____

3. **A:** Movie directors spend too much money on special effects.
    B: You don't know what you're talking about.
More polite response:

_____

ACTIVITY 20 Preparing for group discussion

How would you respond to the following statements/questions? Think about your answers carefully to prepare for the group discussion in Activity 21.

1. Name a few inventions that you think would be difficult to live without (e.g., cell phone).
2. "Necessity is the mother of invention." What do you think this famous proverb means?
3. Which do you enjoy more—blockbuster Hollywood movies or independent, less popular, movies? Why?
4. Do you think movie actors make too much money? Why or why not?
5. Do you think the rating system for movies (G, PG, PG-13, R) is necessary? Why or why not?
6. Have you ever been to Los Angeles/Hollywood? Do you think it's a good tourist destination?

STRATEGY

Taking on Roles in Groups

Before, during, or after lectures, college instructors often have students form groups to problem-solve or to discuss the lecture content or related topics. Instructors know that sometimes one group member can dominate the discussion. To prevent this and to help everyone take an active role during group discussions, each group member will have a specific role. These roles may change throughout the semester. Sometimes your instructor will assign different roles to group members or members will assign themselves roles. Read the duties of each group member.

Leader

Starts the discussion
Makes sure everyone understands the task
Makes sure that all members contribute and that no one
    dominates
Keeps track of time

Reporter

Writes down main points of discussion
Gives an oral summary if required

Participants*

Think about topic being discussed
Contribute ideas
Do not dominate other group members

*There may be more than one participant in each group; sometimes the participants have more chances to speak because they are not busy with the job of leading or reporting.

ACTIVITY 21   Taking on roles in group discussions

Form groups of three or four. Follow these steps:

1. Assign yourselves (or wait for your instructor's assignments) the roles of leader, reporter, and participant(s).
2. Discuss the questions from Activity 20.
3. Reporter—be ready to summarize your group's results to the whole class.

ACTIVITY 22 Evaluating roles in group discussions

Think about your participation in the group discussion in this chapter. Write the answers to these questions on a separate sheet of paper or in an e-mail to your instructor.

Leader

1. What did you do to start the discussion? Did it work well? Why or why not?
2. What did you do to make sure that everyone participated in the discussion?
3. What did you do to make sure that your classmates stayed on topic during the discussion and finished in the allotted time?
4. What will you do differently when you are the group leader again?

Reporter

1. Were you able to write down all the main points of the discussion? Why or why not?
2. What did you do if you didn't understand something your classmates said?
3. If you had to give a report to the entire class, did you think it was effective? Why or why not?
4. What will you do differently when you are the reporter again?

Participant

1. Were you able to contribute your ideas effectively during the group discussion? Why or why not?
2. What did you do to avoid dominating the other participants?
3. What will you do differently when you are a participant again?

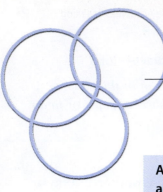

Part 3

ASSESSING YOUR LISTENING AND SPEAKING SKILLS

At the end of each chapter, you will find some tasks that will help you and your instructor evaluate whether you have learned the skills presented in the chapter. In addition, you will find some activities that ask you to reflect on your own progress.

ACTIVITY 23 Identifying syllable number and stress

With a partner, pronounce these words out loud and use the numbering system used in this chapter to indicate how many syllables there are in each word and which syllable is stressed. Ask your instructor to pronounce the words if necessary.

1. distribute [___ - ___]

2. aware [___ - ___]

3. regulate [___ - ___]

4. chronological [___ - ___]

5. guarantee [___ - ___]

6. depression [___ - ___]

7. criteria [___ - ___]

8. compete [___ - ___]

9. responsible [___ - ___]

10. audience [___ - ___]

ACTIVITY 24 **Demonstrating how to take notes**

Listen to your instructor give a short lecture about the movie industry in the first half of the twentieth century. Practice the outline format again to help guide you in preparing for a short answer test. The main ideas for each section are provided.

The Hollywood "Code": Before and After

- After WWI—freedom from morality rules

- Organizations & Regulations

- 1930s and 1940s—popular decade for movies

- By 1950s—Hollywood started challenging the control

ACTIVITY 25 **Responding to short answer questions**

Answer the following questions based on your lecture notes.

1. How did Americans show their sense of freedom after WWI in the way they dressed?
2. In the previous lecture, MPPC stood for Motion Picture Patents Company. What does it stand for in this lecture?
3. What are two aspects of movies that the MPPC banned?
4. In what year was the MPA rating system developed?
5. How much was the fine for directors who did not follow the rules of the MPPC?
6. The MPPDA was considered a "self-regulatory" organization. What does this mean?
7. Give two reasons why movies were so popular during the 1930s and 40s.

ACTIVITY 26 **Reflecting on what you have learned**

Complete the following sentences based on the material and activities from this chapter.

1. One note-taking strategy I want to use in the future is . . .
2. One way I can predict the organization of the lecture is to . . .
3. One way I can predict the content of the lecture is to . . .
4. One way I can make sure I have all the important information in my notes is to . . .
5. One way I can prepare for a short answer test about a lecture is to . . .
6. One way I can be a better participant in a discussion group is to . . .

ACTIVITY 27 **Evaluating your progress**

Listed on the next page are the objectives that were presented at the beginning of the chapter. Read through each one carefully, and evaluate your progress by checking: "Definitely need more help!", "Need a bit more practice!" or "Got it!"

Objectives	Definitely need more help!	Need a bit more practice!	Got it!
Discuss effective note-taking strategies			
Recognize syllable number and stress in academic vocabulary			
Recognize and use signal words of time to organize information from a reading or lecture			
Take notes from a lecture using headings as guides			
Ask classmates clarification questions immediately following a lecture			
Process notes on a chart or timeline			
Predict exam questions from lecture content and reading			
Take on duties as a member of a group discussion			

WEB POWER

You will find additional exercises related to the content in this chapter at http://elt.thomson.com/collegeoral.

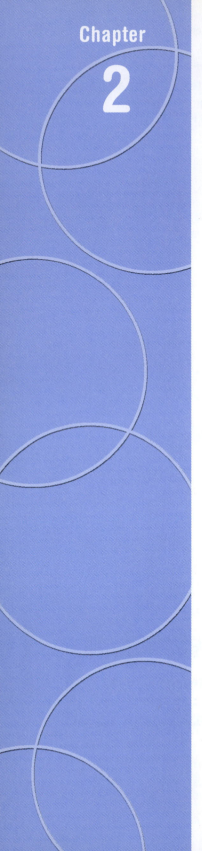

How'd They Do That?

ACADEMIC FOCUS:
COMPUTER SCIENCE ▶ COMPUTER ANIMATION
TECHNOLOGY

Academic Listening and Speaking Objectives

In this chapter, you will continue to develop your skills as an academic listener and speaker. You will work individually, in pairs, and in small groups to:

- Listen for and write down key content, signal, and classroom instruction words
- Use abbreviations when taking notes
- Recognize several syllable stress patterns in academic words
- Recognize language that signals processes in academic reading and lectures
- Use a recall column to make notes more useful
- Predict test questions based on lecture notes
- Give a short "how-to" presentation
- Provide feedback on a classmate's presentation

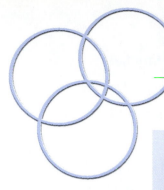

Part 1

EFFECTIVE ACADEMIC LISTENING

In this chapter, you will continue to develop skills that will help you get more accurate information from an academic lecture. You will listen for three different types of keywords. You will also practice using abbreviations to allow you to write down those keywords quickly and use a recall column in your notes. During this chapter, you will work with material that describes the process of creating computer-generated images.

○ Getting Ready for the Lecture

STRATEGY

Recognizing Word Families

Many words belong to a group or "family" of words. This family includes words that have the same basic meaning but different forms according to whether they are nouns, verbs, adjectives, or adverbs. For example, let's look at the word *innovate*. When you learn about the word *innovate*, you should also learn the other forms in the same family, such as the noun(s) and adjective (and adverb, if there is one).

-ate → usually a verb ending	innovate (to begin something new)
-tion, -sion → a noun ending (thing)	innovation (something new)
-er, -or → a noun ending (person)	innovator (person who creates)
-ive → usually an adjective ending	innovative (characterized as something new)

ACTIVITY **1**   **Recognizing different word families**

Circle the correct form of the word in the sentences that follow.

1. The dinosaurs at the museum looked so (*reality / realistic*) that I thought they were actually alive.
2. Computer animators are able to (*transform / transformation*) a human character into a monster using special software.
3. As the (*technology / technological*) of cell phones (*evolution / evolves*), the size of the phone is getting smaller and smaller.
4. Good instructors are always looking for (*innovative / innovate*) techniques to use in the classroom.

STRATEGY

Recognizing Syllable Stress Patterns

Many words have syllable stress that follows certain patterns. Being aware of some of these patterns can help you recognize and say words that may be somewhat unfamiliar to you, even if you do not have a dictionary. There are exceptions to these patterns, but knowing a few of them may help give you more confidence in pronouncing new words.

Type of Word	Pattern	Examples
Most 2-syllable nouns	stress on first syllable	con´text [2-1]
Most 2-syllable verbs	stress on second syllable	create´ [2-2]
Most 3-syllable words ending in: -ate, -ize, -ise	stress on first syllable	an´imate [3-1] in´novate [3-1]
Most 4–5 syllable words ending in: -ate or -ous	stress on second syllable	contin´uous [4-2] commu´nicate [4-2]
Words that end in suffixes such as -ic, -ical, -ual, -tion, -ity, -ogy, -ian, -tal,	stress on syllable preceding suffix	tech´nical [3-2] anima´tion [4-2]
Words that end in suffixes such as -eer and -ee	stress on the final syllable	engineer´ [3-3] guarantee´ [3-3]

ACTIVITY 2 **Predicting the pronunciation of words**

Using the information about syllable stress patterns and the numbering system from Chapter 1, indicate how many syllables there are in each word and which syllable is stressed without using your dictionary. Then listen to the pronunciation of these words and confirm your choices of stress patterns.

1. effort   [—— - ——]

2. graphic   [—— - ——]

3. quantity   [—— - ——]

4. evolution   [—— - ——]   evolve   [—— - ——]

5. innovate   [—— - ——]   innovation   [—— - ——]

6. transformation   [—— - ——]   transform   [—— - ——]

7. technology   [—— - ——]   technological   [—— - ——]

8. reality   [—— - ——]   realistic   [—— - ——]

9. instance   [—— - ——]

10. engineer   [—— - ——]

ACTIVITY 3 Reading material to prepare for lecture

Students usually have reading assignments to prepare for an upcoming lecture. Read the following description of how computer animation is used in movies.

COMPUTER ANIMATION AND THE CINEMA WORLD

Think of the swirls[1] of the bullets that whiz past Neo's shoulder in the *Matrix*, or the slashing motion of Luke Skywalker's sword in George Lucas' *Star Wars* or the laser guns of the alien spaceships in the movie *Independence Day*. All of these scenes have a common ingredient in their recipe for success: all of them look realistic. The world of cinema has evolved over time in able to produce extremely realistic special effects. The quantity and quality of the graphical elements promised by the moviemakers have become more advanced, and as a result have attracted a larger audience. The catalyst[2] behind all of these transformations has been the steady evolution of computer animation technology—blurring[3] the boundaries between art and technology, and resulting in more realistic representations. Behind this advancement are computer animators and engineers.

Every time you watch a movie that uses remarkable computer generated graphics, you probably don't consider the amount of time and effort put into the movie by engineers and scientists. To meet the needs of a particular animated movie scene, engineers sometimes have to create a new chapter of technology by innovating new computer graphic tools. For instance, in creating movies such as *Jurassic Park*, *Antz*, and *A Bug's Life*, engineers had to develop new cinema graphics FX (effects) software packages. Computer animation technology and the film industry are so intertwined[4] that when a movie is being made, you can raise a question similar to the eternal dilemma of the chicken or the egg: "which comes first, the animation technology that is going to be used in the movie or the story of the movie?"

Excerpt from "Computer Animation and the Cinema World," by Mahmooda Sultana, from *Illumin*. Reprinted by permission. For more information: http://illumin.usc.edu

1. *swirls* = something that twists
2. *catalyst* = something that creates changes
3. *blurring* = making unclear
4. *intertwined* = joined together

ACTIVITY 4 **Understanding concepts from the reading**

Answer the following questions on a separate sheet of paper, or discuss the answers in small groups.

1. Do you consider computer-animated movies "art" or "technology" or both?
2. Why do you think there have been so many movies with computer-animated animals?
3. Do you think actors need to worry that computer characters will replace them one day?
4. Why do you think that computer animation takes so much time and effort?

STRATEGY

Recognizing Keywords

Taking notes from lectures (or from instructions) requires you to listen carefully and write quickly. This process includes two important elements:
1. recognizing what is important
2. writing down this information quickly

Content words

Keywords/expressions related directly to the content of the lecture either from the reading, previous lecture, or the current lecture. You should try to be as familiar as possible with these words before the lecture (e.g., MPPC, kinetoscope) through reading or other preparation.

Signal words

Keywords/expressions that help you understand how the instructor is going to organize the lecture (e.g., chronologically, process, or comparison-contrast).

Classroom instruction words

Key content words/expressions used by instructors to announce what s/he expects you to do during or outside of class. These announcements may be made at the beginning of class, in the middle of the lecture (e.g., date of test, material covered on test, homework assignment, date changes, etc.) or at the end of class.

ACTIVITY 5 **Recognizing types of keywords in sentences**

Before we listen to parts of a lecture and classroom instructions, make sure you can recognize different types of keywords. Underline the keywords in the sentences that follow and classify each word as a content, signal, *or* classroom instruction *word. More than one category might apply. Check your answers with a partner. The first one has been done for you.*

1. Around the <u>same time</u> in <u>France</u>, the <u>Lumiere brothers</u> invented the <u>first projector</u>, called the <u>cinematographe</u>, in 1895. Be sure to write this down because you'll need to know all the <u>dates</u> for <u>Friday's quiz</u>.

   Content words: *France, Lumiere brothers,*
   first projector, cinematographe

   Classroom instruction words: *dates, friday's quiz*

   Signal words: *same time, in 1895*

2. So, in 1966, another organization made up of people within the movie industry, developed the MPA, the Motion Picture Association rating system.

   Content words: _____

   _____

   Classroom instruction words: _____

   Signal words: _____

3. There will be six short answer questions on Monday's test. You will have 90 minutes to complete the test.

   Content words: _____

   _____

   Classroom instruction words: _____

   Signal words: _____

4. After the wireframes are created, the animator can then add the shading to the characters.

Content words: _____

_____

Classroom instruction words: _____

Signal words: _____

STRATEGY

Using Verbal/Nonverbal Cues to Recognize Keywords

Now you are more familiar with types of words that are important to write down in your notes. You should also listen or look for cues instructors use during lectures to let you know that these important words are being used. Even though instructors have different styles of speaking, certain techniques are often used to emphasize keywords. When instructors want to call students' attention to something important, they may do one or more of the following:

- change their voice (e.g., talk louder, speak more slowly)
- repeat, spell, or write a word on the board to give you extra time to write something down
- point to specific words/phrases on the blackboard, overhead transparencies, Powerpoint presentations
- pause after saying a word (again, more time to write!)
- use body language by walking closer to the front row of students, leaning forward, using hand gestures, etc.

ACTIVITY 6   Writing down keywords from lectures

Listen to the following excerpts from a lecture. Circle the keywords based on the verbal cues you hear. The first one is done for you.

1. By using software, the animator can add (color), (bumps), and (hair) to make the characters appear alive. That's three things: [pause] (color), (bumps), and (hair).
2. The third very crucial step is called rendering. That's r-e-n-d-e-r-i-n-g.
3. This is called wireframe. [pause] The process is called wireframing.
4. Each second of film has twenty-four frames.

S T R A T E G Y

Using Abbreviations in Lecture Notes

In addition to writing down keywords, good note-takers have a collection of abbreviations they use to help them write more quickly. It's important to abbreviate these words in a way you can recognize them later in your review. Here are some tips to consider when using abbreviations.* Notice that more than one strategy is often used.

Use first syllable and first letter of second syllable OR first and second syllable:

> effects → *eff.*   information → *info.*

Use 's to signify plurals, 'g to signify -ing endings, 'l to signify -al endings, 'r to signify -er endings:

> establishing → *establish'g*   filmmaker → *filmk'r*

Drop vowels:

> graphic → *grphc.*   movement → *mvmt.*

Use initials for key terms that are repeated in a lecture:

> Motion Picture Association *MPA*
> computer generated imagery *CGI*

Use conventional abbreviations when possible:

> pages *pp.*   for example *e.g.*   Thursday *Th.*

*Go to the Thomson Heinle website for examples of other abbreviations.

ACTIVITY 7 Creating abbreviations for key content words

The words in the following list could be used in lectures/readings about computer animation. You will hear these words many times, so having abbreviations for them will be helpful. Decide how you would abbreviate each one, using the strategies from the preceding box. Keep in mind that you probably will use a combination of strategies for many words.

1. animator   = ___animt'r___

2. wireframe   = _____

3. technique   = _____

4. three-dimensional = _____

5. special effects   = _____

6. digital   = _____

7. traditionally   = _____

8. manipulating   = _____

ACTIVITY 8 Writing down keywords using abbreviations

Listen to a few sentences from the upcoming lecture. Write down keywords by using abbreviations.

Master Student Tip

If the professor repeats the same keywords or phrase several times during a lecture, it is important to highlight or underline these in your notes.

You will hear:

Digitizing takes place in the post-production stage.

You could write: Digitiz'g–pst. prdction stg.

1. _____

2. _____

3. _____

POWER GRAMMAR

Recognizing Signal Words of Process

Successful students recognize when an instructor is pointing out the steps in a process. In Chapter 1, you listened for signal words of chronology. In the reading and lecture you will hear, you will learn about steps that are taken when creating digital characters for movies. To point out these steps, these keywords/expressions of process may be used:

First(ly),...	Second(ly),...	Third(ly),...
To start,...	Then,...	Next,...
To begin (with),...	Finally,...	Afterwards,...
The first/second/ third step is...	Once X is done,...	When...
Turning now.../ Let's turn to...	Having looked at X, let's turn to...	Moving on...

ACTIVITY 9 Listening for signal words of process

Listen to the sentences from the lecture. Identify whether you think the excerpt indicates the beginning, middle, or end of a process.

You will hear:

After the wireframes are created, the animator can add shading to the models.

beginning (middle) end

1. beginning middle end

2. beginning middle end

3. beginning middle end

4. beginning middle end

> **Master Student Tip**
>
> It's important to concentrate on what your instructor is saying throughout the entire lecture. Do not let your mind wander or get distracted; you may miss essential information.

○ Getting Information from a Lecture

Listening to a lecture should not be a passive activity. It takes energy, but successful students learn to use different types of note-taking techniques to become "active listeners." In the upcoming lecture, you will use a technique developed at Cornell University, which involves using a recall column in your notes.

STRATEGY

Using a Recall Column in Your Notes

When you use a recall column, you write your regular notes (main ideas and indented details using symbols and abbreviations) on the right side of the paper. On the left, in the recall column, you write keywords and questions during and after the lecture. The division of the paper looks like this.

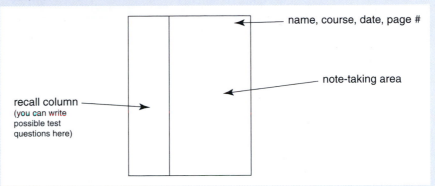

name, course, date, page #

note-taking area

recall column
(you can write possible test questions here)

There are several advantages to using this technique:

- your notes are more organized
- you listen more actively while taking notes because you anticipate questions
- you create a study guide while you are taking notes to save you time later
- you can find information more quickly when you start preparing for a test

How to use this system:

1. Draw a vertical line toward the left-hand side leaving about $\frac{2}{3}$ on the right and $\frac{1}{3}$ on the left.
2. Put your name, course, date, and page number at the top of each new page.
3. Take notes on the right hand side (use the note-taking techniques you learned in Chapters 1 and 2).
4. As soon as you can, review your notes on the right. Compare them with another classmate.
5. Look for keywords, key names, questions, etc., and put them in the recall column on the left.
6. Use the recall column to help you study for your tests.

ACTIVITY 10   Taking complete notes

This lecture focuses on that time in the movie's production when animators create digital characters for a movie. This lecture is divided into steps. Your instructor will decide how many parts of the lecture to work with before you stop to review your notes. Use abbreviations and symbols to write down keywords. Leave the recall column blank for now.

Questions/Comments	Notes
	Uses for comp. anim.
	Comp. anim. and media
	CGI =
	1st step in process

	Creat'g comp. charctrs from humans
	2nd step
	3rd step
	final step
	Review

○ Making Your Notes Useful

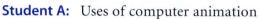 **ACTIVITY** **11** **Reconstructing notes**

Imagine that a classmate asked to borrow your notes and had some questions about what you had written. With a partner, take turns going through each section of your notes and reconstruct full sentences (orally):

Student A: Uses of computer animation
CGI
Creating characters from humans
3rd step in process
Student B: Computer animation and media
1st step in process
2nd step
Final step

Example:

*Information from
your notes*

> Movie drct'rs rely on comp. animat'rs
>   Enhance bkgd. scenery
>   Create chrct'rs
>   Ex: Toy Story I, II,
>   Jurassic Park, Star Wars

*What you can say
to your partner*

> "Many movie directors rely on computer animators to make their movies. For instance, computer animators may enhance background scenery in a movie or even create new characters. Some examples of characters are in movies like the Toy Story movies, Jurassic Park, Star Wars, etc."

ACTIVITY 12 **Filling in the recall column**

Look at the model below with notes from the beginning of the lecture. The recall column is being filled in with questions and comments from the notes on the right. With a partner, look through the notes that each of you took in Activity 10. Decide together which questions and keywords you think should be included in your recall column.

Questions/Comments	Notes
What are some fields that use computer animation?	airlines, military, med.-use comp. anim. for training purposes Architecture-to speed up designs
Why do movie directors use computer animation?	Movie dirct'rs rely on comp. animat'rs Enhance bkgd. scenery Create chrct'rs
Examples of movies with comp. animation	Successful movies with 3-D chrct'rs/machines Toy Story I, II, Jurassic Park, Star Wars, Bug's Life
What does CGI stand for?	CGI = computer-generated imagery

ACTIVITY 13 **Predicting questions for a test**

An advantage to having a recall column in your notes is that you can predict what some of the questions might be on a test. In Chapter 1, you predicted why, when, who, what, where, *and* how *questions based on the lecture. Look at your recall column in Activity 10 and predict five questions you think might appear on a test.*

1. _____

2. _____

3. _____

4. _____

5. _____

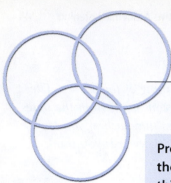

Part 2

EFFECTIVE ACADEMIC SPEAKING

Presentations often follow patterns that are similarly organized to the lectures you hear, although the length may be much shorter. In this chapter, you are going to prepare a short presentation on how to do something.

○ Preparing a Presentation

There are steps in preparing for a presentation. Following these steps helps effective students succeed in conveying their information to their audience.

1. Understand the assignment well
   a. analyze your audience
   b. understand the presentation's purpose (to demonstrate, inform, analyze, etc.)
   c. read the class syllabus carefully to see what you are expected to do

2. Choose and narrow down your topic
   a. choose a topic that interests you (or else you'll struggle through the process!)
   b. find out the time limit
   c. write focus questions and/or brainstorm to narrow topic
   d. concentrate on a specific topic with one main idea
   e. ask questions during class or office hours to be sure you understand

3. Gather information and plan your outline
   a. state your purpose
   b. choose your main points
   c. describe each main point with facts, illustrations, examples
   d. prepare your conclusion
   e. prepare your introduction

4. Deliver your presentation
   a. speak from note cards, but don't read them
   b. never apologize
   c. keep track of time
   d. look at audience

STRATEGY

Preparing an Outline (Example)

Topic:

How are newspapers printed?

Focus questions/brainstorming to narrow topic:

a. What machines are used?
b. How many people are needed?
c. What are the steps?
d. How long does it take?

Purpose:

to explain how a newspaper is printed using a printing press

Main points:*

Printing process includes:

a. stories and photos are sent to the production department of a newspaper
b. images/articles are put onto aluminum plates
c. information on plates is transferred to rubber rollers
d. rubber rollers with ink print information onto paper
e. large presses also cut and put pages in order

Conclusion:

To conclude, although news is readily available on television and the Internet, newspapers have survived as a daily source of information for many people. The process of printing newspapers will probably change as the technology changes. Understanding the process helps us appreciate the daily paper found in the coin box on the corner or delivered to our houses every day.

Introduction/interesting fact/idea for introduction to interest the audience:

Although newspapers are no longer the most popular way for people to get their news, there are still more than 1,600 newspapers printed daily in the United States, and the steps in their production are quite interesting. Producing a daily newspaper involves a lot of people and major machinery, so today I would like to explain the process of printing a newspaper.

*Each of these main points should also include supporting details to help the audience understand the information.

ACTIVITY 14   **Preparing an oral presentation on a process**

The topic for this presentation is to explain a process or everyday phenomenon that many people may be familiar with but not completely understand. You will deliver this first four to six minute presentation to one or two other students. Go to the Thomson Heinle website for this chapter and choose a topic that interests you.

Sample Topics

- how a computer virus spreads
- how a CD burner works

Use this outline to help you plan your presentation.

Topic:

Focus questions/brainstorming to narrow topic:

Purpose:

Main points:

Conclusion:

Introduction (include interesting fact/idea for introduction to interest the audience):

POWER GRAMMAR

Pronouncing Final -s in Academic Speaking

To make yourself clearly understood when giving a presentation, it is important to pronounce the final -s on words. For example, plural nouns, possessives, simple present verbs in third person, and contractions need to be pronounced clearly to avoid confusion.

> Large ship**S** arrive in Miami every day. (plural)
> The ship'**S** captain is named Darrell Warren. (possessive)
> My mother always ship**S** boxes of clothes to me. (verb)
> The cruise ship'**S** leaving at 9:00 a.m. (contraction)

If a word ends in a voiceless consonant, the ending is pronounced /s/.

> **caps, laughs, pats, breaths, bricks**

If a word ends in a voiced consonant or vowel, the ending is pronounced /z/.

> **tabs, rooms, curves, lines, balls, lids, tags, bangs, breathes, trays, flies**

If a word ends in /s/, /z/, /ʃ/, /tʃ/, or /dʒ/, the ending is pronounced /ɪz/.

> **buses, roses, wishes, witches, nudges**

ACTIVITY 15 **Pronouncing final -s**

Determine how to pronounce each of the final -s sounds in the following words. With a partner, take turns pronouncing the complete sentences, paying close attention to the underlined words.

1. A journalist's job is to write interesting articles about the news.

   (/s/, /z/, /ɪz/)   (/s/, /z/, /ɪz/)   (/s/, /z/, /ɪz/)

2. Journalist's send their stories to the various departments.

   (/s/, /z/, /ɪz/)   (/s/, /z/, /ɪz/)   (/s/, /z/, /ɪz/)

3. Large presses cut and put the pages in order.

   (/s/, /z/, /ɪz/)   (/s/, /z/, /ɪz/)

4. Printing's changing as the technology changes.

   (/s/, /z/, /ɪz/)   (/s/, /z/, /ɪz/)

Master Student Tip

Don't memorize something you have written in paragraph form. It will sound artificial. Talk to your audience ... not at them.

ACTIVITY 16 **Delivering a presentation**

Before presenting your information, review the guidelines and sample in previous activities and the peer review chart in Activity 17. Sit with one or two other students and deliver your presentation.

ACTIVITY 17 **Peer reviewing a classmate's presentation**

Fill out this chart and answer these questions about your classmate's presentation. Discuss your answers with your classmate.

Presentation: Peer Review			
Speaker: _____ **Topic:** _____			
Did your classmate . . .			
1. state the presentation's main purpose in the introduction?	Yes	Somewhat	No
2. present three to five main points (steps of process)?	Yes	Somewhat	No
3. present steps in logical order?	Yes	Somewhat	No
4. present enough information for you to understand each step?	Yes	Somewhat	No
5. use signal words of process between each step?	Yes	Somewhat	No
6. explain any words that you may not know?	Yes	Somewhat	No
7. include a conclusion summarizing her/his main points?	Yes	Somewhat	No
8. keep track of time?	Yes	Somewhat	No
9. speak without reading word for word from her/his notes?	Yes	Somewhat	No
10. pronounce final -s endings clearly?	Yes	Somewhat	No
11. speak loudly enough?	Yes	Somewhat	No
12. seem prepared?	Yes	Somewhat	No

What was the strongest aspect of this speaker's presentation?

What suggestions for improvement do you have for the speaker?

What would you like to use from this speaker's presentation in your next presentation?

Part 3

ASSESSING YOUR LISTENING AND SPEAKING SKILLS

At the end of each chapter, you will find some tasks that will help you and your instructor evaluate whether you have learned the skills presented in the chapter. In addition, you will find some activities that ask you to reflect on your own progress.

ACTIVITY 18   Giving a short presentation

Evaluate the peer review information from your partner. Revise your presentation and deliver it to the whole class (or as directed by your instructor).

◯ Assessing Your Speaking

Your instructor may use this checklist to evaluate your use of academic English in your speaking assignments.

Speaker: _____ Topic: _____	Outstanding (5)	(4)	OK (3)	(2)	Poor (1)
1. Speaker states the presentation's main purpose in the introduction.					
2. Speaker presents three to five main points (steps of process).					
3. Speaker presents steps in logical order.					
4. Speaker presents enough information for the audience to understand each step.					
5. Speaker uses signal words of process between each step.					
6. Speaker explains any words that the audience may not know.					
7. Speaker's conclusion summarized her/his main points.					
8. Speaker keeps track of time.					
9. Speaker talks without reading word for word from her/his notes.					
10. Speaker pronounces final -s endings clearly.					
11. Speaker is loud enough.					
12. Speaker seems prepared.					

Comments:

ACTIVITY 19 **Listening to a lecture and taking notes**

Listen to another part of the process of putting special effects into movies. Take notes using the outline that follows.

Questions/Comments	Notes
	Movie Production Stages Bckgd. 1st stage- Teams & Assignmnts. 2nd stage Final stage

ACTIVITY 20 Interpreting a classmate's notes

When a good student is absent from class, she/he borrows someone else's notes as soon as possible to obtain the necessary information. Imagine that you were absent from the lecture in Activity 19. Exchange notes with a partner and see if you can fill in her/his recall column with main ideas and/or study questions. Ask each other questions if necessary.

ACTIVITY 21 Reflecting on what you have learned

Complete the following sentences based on the material and activities from this chapter.

1. The note-taking strategies I'm more comfortable using now are . . .

2. The three different types of keywords are . . .

3. Two syllable stress patterns I will remember are . . .

4. The major reason to use abbreviations while taking notes is . . .

5. A few signal words that an instructor uses when explaining a process are . . .

6. One advantage of using a recall column in my notes is . . .

7. One important step in preparing a presentation is . . .

8. One thing I learned about giving an oral presentation is . . .

9. One aspect I'd like to improve for future presentations is . . .

ACTIVITY 22 **Evaluating your progress**

Listed below are the objectives that were presented at the beginning of Chapter 2. Read each one carefully and evaluate your progress by checking: "Definitely need more help!", "Need a bit more practice!" or "Got it!"

Objectives	Definitely need more help!	Need a bit more practice!	Got it!
Listen for and write down key content, signal, and classroom instruction words			
Use abbreviations when taking notes			
Recognize several syllable stress patterns in academic words			
Recognize language that signals processes in academic reading and lectures			
Use a recall column to make notes more useful			
Predict test questions based on lecture notes			
Give a short "how-to" presentation			
Provide feedback on classmate's presentation			

WEB POWER

You will find additional exercises related to the content in this chapter at **http://elt.thomson.com/collegeoral**.

Can You Hear Me Now?

ACADEMIC FOCUS:
SOCIAL SCIENCES ▶ COMMUNICATION STUDIES

Academic Listening and Speaking Objectives

In this chapter, you will continue to develop your skills as an academic listener and speaker. You will work individually, in pairs, and in small groups to:

- Recognize and use signal words of comparison
- Use symbols to note keywords
- Recognize syllable stress patterns in academic words
- Predict reading focus from diagrams and text
- Use signal words of comparison to include graphic organizers in notes
- Use notes to create concept cards
- Predict short essay exam questions and write effective answers
- Practice working in productive study groups
- Present oral summary of lecture notes
- Leave effective voicemail messages for your instructors

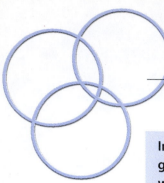

Part 1

EFFECTIVE ACADEMIC LISTENING

In this chapter, you will continue to develop skills that will help you get more accurate information from an academic lecture. You will work with a reading/diagrams describing communication models and then listen to a lecture that compares two different communication processes: interpersonal and mass communication.

○ Getting Ready for the Lecture

ACTIVITY 1 Preparing for the content of a lecture

Every day, we are constantly engaged in different forms of communication. We usually communicate face-to-face with many people. This is called interpersonal communication. These are the conversations with our friends, family, and co-workers. This also includes the telephone calls and e-mail messages we send. In addition to interpersonal communication, we are also constantly "talking" to ourselves in our minds. This is called intrapersonal communication. Lastly, mass communication refers to using many of the devices and materials to communicate to millions of people simultaneously. Each image on this page shows an example of interpersonal, intrapersonal, and mass communication. Can you identify each one? Which one do you prefer to use to communicate with other people?

ACTIVITY 2 Preparing for the content of a lecture

Work with a partner and discuss whether each of these situations is an example of interpersonal, intrapersonal, or mass communication.

1. Waving hello to one of your classmates across the street
2. Sending an e-mail message to your instructor to tell her you're sick
3. Writing a letter to a friend
4. Talking to your mom on your cell phone
5. Listening to the radio on the beach
6. Watching CNN, Headline, or Fox News every morning
7. Arguing with your spouse about who should take out the garbage
8. Thinking to yourself, "I need to lose five pounds by summer."
9. Inputting your dentist appointment on your Palm Pilot
10. Reading highway billboards on the way to work

STRATEGY

Using a Dictionary to Learn Pronunciation of New Words, Word Families, and Accurate Meanings

Dictionaries offer a lot of information about a single word. You can find the number of syllables and stress, the different meanings, and the word's other forms. Look at the different parts of the following dictionary entry.

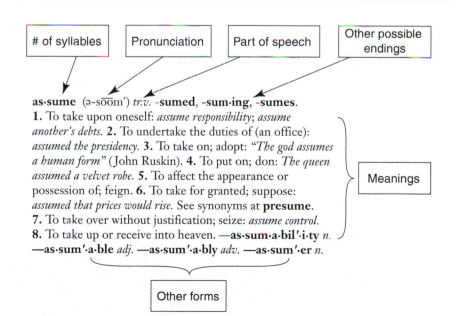

| # of syllables | Pronunciation | Part of speech | Other possible endings |

as·sume (ə-sōōm′) *tr.v.* **-sumed, -sum·ing, -sumes.**
1. To take upon oneself: *assume responsibility*; *assume another's debts.* **2.** To undertake the duties of (an office): *assumed the presidency.* **3.** To take on; adopt: *"The god assumes a human form"* (John Ruskin). **4.** To put on; don: *The queen assumed a velvet robe.* **5.** To affect the appearance or possession of; feign. **6.** To take for granted; suppose: *assumed that prices would rise.* See synonyms at **presume.** **7.** To take over without justification; seize: *assume control.* **8.** To take up or receive into heaven. —**as·sum·a·bil′·i·ty** *n.* —**as·sum′·a·ble** *adj.* —**as·sum′·a·bly** *adv.* —**as·sum′·er** *n.*

Meanings

Other forms

ACTIVITY 3 **Using a dictionary for stress and meaning**

Use a dictionary to look up the underlined words in the sentences that follow. Answer the questions based on the dictionary entry. The first one has been done for you.

1. The instructor walked into the classroom and said, "I <u>assume</u> that you are all curious about how you did on last week's exam."

    a. Which syllable is stressed? _the 2nd_

    b. Which meaning best fits the sentence above? _#6, to take for granted; suppose_

    c. What part of speech is *assume*? _verb_

    d. What is the adjective form of *assume*? _assumable_

2. It is much easier for people to <u>transmit</u> diseases due to the amount of air travel we do.

    a. What part of speech is *transmit*? _____

    b. What is the adjective form of *transmit*? _____

    c. Which meaning best fits the sentence above? _____

    _____

3. My new dress has an <u>elaborate</u> pattern of flowers and lace.

    a. What part of speech is *elaborate*? _____

    b. What is the noun (person) form of *elaborate*? _____

    c. Which meaning best fits the sentence above? _____

    _____

ACTIVITY 4   Predicting the pronunciation of content words

Using the information about syllable stress patterns and the numbering system in Chapters 1 and 2, indicate how many syllables there are in each word and which syllable is stressed.

1. initiate   [___ - ___]   initiation   [___ - ___]
2. destination   [___ - ___]
3. elaborate   [___ - ___]   elaboration   [___ - ___]
4. message   [___ - ___]
5. transmission   [___ - ___]   transmit   [___ - ___]
6. assumption   [___ - ___]   assume   [___ - ___]
7. geographic   [___ - ___]
8. recur   [___ - ___]
9. emphasize   [___ - ___]
10. economic   [___ - ___]
11. mediate   [___ - ___]   mediation   [___ - ___]
12. creativity   [___ - ___]   create   [___ - ___]
13. collaborate   [___ - ___]   collaboration   [___ - ___]

ACTIVITY 5   Predicting the focus of a reading

Scan through the reading (look at the diagrams and topic sentences of the paragraphs) and answer the following questions.

1. What do you think the purpose of this reading is?
2. How many different models of communication are presented in the reading?
3. Who are the creators of the models mentioned in the reading?
4. In which year was each model created?
5. Which terms are used in more than one model?
6. Which model includes the concept of "noise"?

ACTIVITY 6 **Reading material to prepare for the lecture**

Read the following description of different models of communication. Be sure to review the graphic representations of each model.

MODELS OF HUMAN COMMUNICATION

There have been several models of human communication developed over the years to help us better understand the process. Although the creators of the models came from different backgrounds and had different purposes for designing their models, many of the basic components have remained constant.

One of the first models was developed by a political scientist named Harold Lasswell. In 1947, Lasswell worked with a group of sociologists who were also interested in the effects of mass communication. Lasswell was the first to introduce several components that recur in later models.

Lasswell's Model

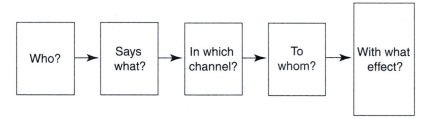

A few years later in 1949, an employee of Bell Telephone Company named Claude Shannon and a mathematician named Warren Weaver designed a model similar to Lasswell's, but theirs was more technical. This model, which is based on telephone technology, is often presented in first year introductory communication courses.

Shannon-Weaver Model

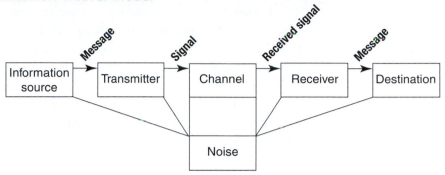

Like Lasswell's model, this graphic representation also emphasizes the linear characteristic of the communication process. In the Shannon-Weaver model, an information source (e.g., an idea in your head) initiates a message. This message is passed on through a transmitter (e.g., your mouth) and sent via a signal (e.g., your voice) to a receiver. Then the receiver (e.g., listener's ear) conveys the message to the final destination (e.g., listener's mind). Before reaching the receiver, however, the message most likely encounters physical noise (e.g., interference such as a loud crowd in a restaurant) or semantic noise (distraction such as a speaker's beautiful smile). The Shannon-Weaver model was the first to recognize the possible influence of this noise. However, both models are based on the concept of transmission; the message flows in one direction.

A model that takes a different perspective is attributed to Wilbur Schramm and others with whom he collaborated in the mid 1960s. This model is much different from Shannon-Weaver's because it concentrates on the individuals and what they have in common rather than on how the message is sent (channel).

Schramm's Model

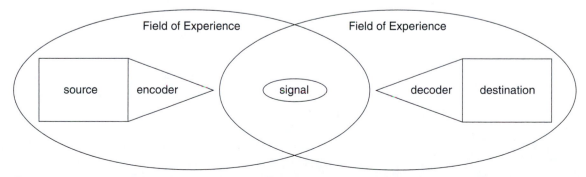

In this model, the different components such as the source and destination are clearly depicted, but the concept of encoder and decoder are also included. According to Schramm, messages need to be encoded (in writing, speaking, printing, or filming) using common symbols in the same "field of experience" for both the source and destination. If not, the message will not be understood. For example, a parent might encode the word "candy" to the other parent by spelling it (C-A-N-D-Y) so that their two-year-old cannot understand it. The parents have a common "field of experience" that is not shared by the two-year-old.

Although the models differ in some ways, many of the same terms are used to describe the communication process.

POWER GRAMMAR

Recognizing Words that Signal Comparisons

During a lecture or reading, effective students recognize when similarities and differences between different ideas are emphasized. The reading presented three models of communication; in the lecture you will hear, your instructor will compare interpersonal communication and mass communication. To point out the similarities and differences, the following words/expressions can be used:

Words/Phrases Signaling Similarities	Words/Phrases Signaling Differences
too	but
also	in contrast
similar to	whereas
both	on the other hand
likewise	unlike
in the same way	however
similarly	different from
the same	yet
as well as	while

ACTIVITY 7 **Showing understanding of the reading**

Form groups of three and write five (5) sentences that point out similarities and differences among the Lasswell, Shannon-Weaver, and Schramm models that you read about in Activity 6. Do not copy sentences directly from the reading; discuss the ideas in your group and write them in your own words. The first one has been done for you.

1. Unlike Lasswell's and Schramm's model, the Shannon-Weaver model shows how "noise" can affect communication.

2. _____

3. _____

4. _____

5. _____

6. _____

ACTIVITY 8 Recognizing signal words of comparison

Listen to the following sentences from the upcoming lecture and decide whether your instructor is talking about a similarity or a difference between different ideas.

You will hear:

In both interpersonal and mass communication, messages are sent to entertain, to inform, or to persuade.

You should circle:

(similarity)   difference

1. similarity   difference

2. similarity   difference

3. similarity   difference

4. similarity   difference

5. similarity   difference

6. similarity   difference

7. similarity   difference

8. similarity   difference

Using Graphic Organizers

Listening to signal words of comparison can often lead effective note-takers to make graphic organizers during a lecture to help organize the information. Charts, diagrams, or tables clearly show the differences (and sometimes similarities) between two different ideas. The diagrams that follow can be adapted for the lecture for this chapter.

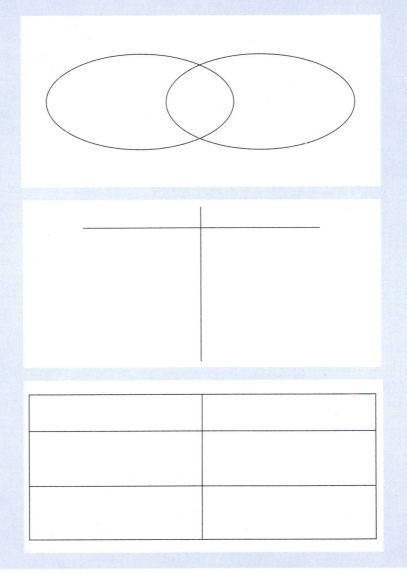

ACTIVITY 9 Listening for signal words to draw charts

Listening for signal words of comparison can also help you organize your notes. When you hear these key signal words, you can quickly organize your notes and include graphic organizers.

Read along and listen to the example that follows. The information for mass communication has been filled in. Finish the chart with the information for interpersonal communication.

You will hear:

Let's move on to the channel, which if you remember from Lasswell's and Shannon-Weaver's models means how the message is sent—the path. In mass communication, there are many types of channels. The path of the message can go through a variety of media, such as print or film. There is also an economic influence to mass communication channels as well that doesn't exist in interpersonal communication. For example, organizations with more money have the power to send messages through more than one channel. Channels are different in interpersonal communication. Since this type of communication is usually face-to-face, the channel is usually our voice. However, there are also nonverbal factors. For example, feeling someone's touch and even smelling their perfume play a role.

	Mass Communication	**Interpersonal Communication**
Channel = how message is sent (path)	Choices of paths (media) ↓ print ↓ film Econ. infl (more $$, more channels)	

STRATEGY

Using Symbols

In Chapter 2, we looked at using abbreviations to save time when taking notes. Using symbols can also help. Although many students have very individual collections of symbols, some standard symbols are easy to use and recognize:

#	number	w/	with
→	leads to	w/o	without
←	comes from	*	see note below
+	and	=	is, similar to
≈	approximately	≠	is not, different from
re:	regarding	…	continues
<	less than	b/c	because
>	greater than	∴	therefore
vs.	against	?	question

Look at the previous activity and discuss the symbols and abbreviations that were used. Would you have used the same ones? Can you add any symbols or abbreviations?

ACTIVITY 10 **Sharing useful symbols with your classmates**

Although most students share many note-taking strategies, the process also has a very personal touch. Some students have many symbols that they use that other students might not know or think about using. In groups, share different symbols you might all be able to use in your notes. Include the meaning of each symbol so you can refer back to it later.

Symbol	Meaning
☺ or ☹	advantage or disadvantage
_____	_____
_____	_____
_____	_____
_____	_____
_____	_____

◯ Getting Information from a Lecture

> **POWER GRAMMAR**
>
> ### Differentiating Between Content and Function Words
>
> During any kind of speaking, the important words of the sentence are stressed because these are the words that normally transmit the message. They are called *content words* because they contain the important ideas—they are usually nouns, verbs, adjectives, and adverbs. In academic lectures, professors stress the content words. On the other hand, words that are not important to the message's main idea are often reduced (not pronounced completely or clearly). These are called *function words* because they are necessary for correct grammar (articles, pronouns, prepositions, auxiliary verbs, and conjunctions), but not important for the message. When you listen to lectures, therefore, it's important for you to focus on the content words.

ACTIVITY 11 Recognizing content and function word stress

Using the information from the previous box, underline the content words in the sentences that follow. Then, rewrite the information as if you were hearing the sentences in a lecture, using symbols and abbreviations when possible.

1. Mass communication, on the other hand, is the production and distribution of an identical message to a very large and diverse audience using some sort of technology.
   Notes:

2. Encoding also takes place in mass communication messages.
   Notes:

3. There is much less individual control in mass communication than in interpersonal communication.
   Notes:

ACTIVITY 12 Connecting ideas from reading to lecture

Instructors often begin a class session by engaging students in questions related to the outside reading. This is a good way for her/him to check whether the students have read the material and also to make sure that students understand vocabulary and simple concepts before applying the information in a lecture. Listen and write answers to the following questions that an instructor might ask after a reading assignment, or before delivering a lecture.

1. _____

_____

2. _____

_____

3. _____

_____

4. _____

_____

5. _____

_____

6. _____

_____

7. _____

_____

8. _____

_____

ACTIVITY 13 **Taking complete notes**

This lecture focuses on describing the differences between interpersonal and mass communication. The lecture is divided into sections. Your instructor will decide how many parts of the lecture to work with before you stop to review your notes. Incorporate graphic organizers into your notes. Use abbreviations and symbols to write down keywords.

Questions/Comments	Notes

	Differences between interpersonal and mass communication
	
	Def. & Ex.
	
	    Interpers.
	
	    Mass
	
	Similar Components
	  A.
	  B.
	  C.
	  D.
	
		Source

	Message/Encoding
	Recv'r
	Noise
	Info. for Midterm

◯ Making Your Notes Useful

Effective students have strategies for using their notes to study for short essay exams. They usually rewrite the lecture information so that it is neater and easier to read. Other students have more elaborate techniques to also help them remember the information.

STRATEGY

Making and Using Concept Cards

Concept cards are one way to rewrite your notes and create an effective study tool. Instead of reading and rereading notes and textbook material, successful students put the important information on index cards or small sheets of paper to help them memorize it. They also use their own words in writing the information to help them remember it better. When using the cards to study for an exam, one way to be more efficient is to put the cards you have already memorized in a separate pile. This gives you more time to continue studying the concepts that are giving you difficulty. Then return the other cards to the stack and continue the memorization.

Sample Concept Cards

front of card	front of card
Interpersonal communication vs. Mediated interpersonal communication	Channel Interpersonal vs. Mass communication
back of card	**back of card**
= usually face-to-face communication with another person = not face-to-face (something like phone or e-mail in between)	IP = face-to-face; voice and nonverbal factors (e.g. touch and smell) MC = sent through many media (print, film, broadcast)

ACTIVITY 14   Making concept cards to study for an exam

Get a stack of index cards or divide blank sheets of paper into quarters or eighths. Choose ten concepts from the lecture that you think are important. Write a concept card for each one.

ACTIVITY 15   Using concept cards to memorize information

Give your stack of cards to a partner. Take turns "testing" each other on the information. Try to memorize the information on at least five of the ten cards. Save your cards for Activities 17 and 19.

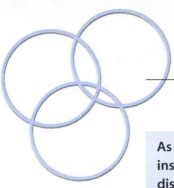

Part 2

EFFECTIVE ACADEMIC SPEAKING

As explained in Chapter 1, sometimes during or after a lecture an instructor may put students into smaller groups so that they can discuss lecture content and the outside reading. Some instructors also do this to encourage students to get to know each other and perhaps form study groups throughout the semester outside of class. In this section, you are going to be involved in several groups. We're going to talk about the importance of such groups and about how to participate effectively as a member.

STRATEGY

Being a Part of a Study Group

In most of your academic classes, studying in groups inside and outside of class can be an effective way to learn the required information. There are many advantages to working in study groups:

- You get immediate feedback from others about whether you understand information
- You develop communication skills that are helpful for the academic and the working worlds
- You get motivated to study earlier for a test than you might normally have
- You can share problems you're having (i.e., talk together as a "support group")

Several different tasks can be done in study groups. The instructor often assigns questions for the group to discuss. However, you and your study group can do other tasks to help each other:

- Summarize the material in the readings/lecture
- Predict questions for an upcoming test
- Write questions you want to ask about the previous lecture
- Come up with memory/visual aids to help you prepare for a test
- Assign members to bring in outside material related to the topic

Each group member usually has to take on responsibility for doing something to "teach" the rest of the group. In this way, your group is depending on you to do your share of the work.

ACTIVITY 16   Working in productive study groups

The next several activities will take place in groups. Write an "E" by the statements that describe efficient study groups and an "I" by those that describe inefficient study groups. Be prepared to explain the reasons for your answers.

1. _____ Each group member listens actively to the others by maintaining eye contact, asking questions if necessary, and giving each person a chance to contribute.

2. _____ One or two talkative people, who usually have very good ideas, are the only ones to participate in the discussion.

3. _____ In groups of four or more, two conversations going on at the same time is OK.

4. _____ Each person is given an opportunity to talk.

5. _____ All the group members have a common goal and understand what that goal is.

6. _____ The discussion topics jump around to whatever interests the current speaker.

ACTIVITY 17   Summarizing the lecture in study groups

> **Master Student Tip**
>
> Don't just memorize facts; try to understand the concepts. When summarizing information for other classmates, try to remember the ideas like stories; pretend you're telling what happened on your favorite TV show or of a great goal in a soccer game.

Now that you've reflected on the usefulness of study groups, in groups of three, take turns orally summarizing the different parts of the lecture that are noted below. Use your notes, but don't just read them. Be sure to listen carefully to your group members, asking more clarification questions (see Chapter 1) if necessary. Add any missing information to your notes.

Group Member #1
- **a.** define interpersonal communication
- **b.** compare source in interpersonal and mass communication

Group Member #2
- **c.** define mass communication
- **d.** compare receiver in interpersonal and mass communication

Group Member #3
- **e.** compare noise in interpersonal and mass communication
- **f.** compare message in interpersonal and mass communication

ACTIVITY 18 Understanding short essay exam words

Taking good notes, making concept cards, and participating productively in study groups are all effective strategies for preparing for short essay exams. Another strategy is to predict questions you think might be on a short answer exam. First, let's make sure that you understand the meaning of short essay exam words. Match each "question" word with the appropriate paraphrased question.

1. _____ Contrast **a.** What is the meaning of . . . ?

2. _____ Compare **b.** How does . . . ?

3. _____ Describe **c.** What are the differences between X and Y?

4. _____ Define **d.** What are the similarities and differences between X and Y?

5. _____ Explain **e.** What are the characteristics of . . . ?

ACTIVITY 19 Predicting short answer questions

Stay in the same study groups in which you completed the oral summaries. Use your notes and concept cards to predict five (5) short answer questions. Start each question with one of the following words: compare, contrast, describe, define, list, *or* explain.

1. _____

2. _____

3. _____

4. _____

5. _____

STRATEGY

Controlling the Talk Time in Group Discussions

When you are participating in a group discussion, it is important for all members to be responsible for keeping the discussion moving and making sure everyone participates. Here are some expressions that can be used by all group members for effective discussions. Can you think of other expressions to add to the different categories?

Clarifying what someone else said:

Do you mean that . . . ?
What do you mean?
Can you explain what you just said?
So what you're saying is that . . . ?

Clarifying what you have said:

What I mean is/said was . . .
Let me repeat what I said.
I think you misunderstood me.

Getting others to talk:

_____, what do you think?
Do you agree or disagree?
Let's hear from someone who (dis)agrees.

Getting others to stop talking:

Maybe _____ has something to add.

ACTIVITY 20 **Answering discussion questions**

Using the group member roles that were introduced in Chapter 1, discuss the following questions concerning the readings, lecture, and your experience with interpersonal and mass communication. Try using expressions from the previous box.

1. Why are many of us willing to pay $50 or more to see a live concert but only about $15 for a CD by the same singer/group? How is this related to the different components of communication?

2. It was mentioned in the lecture that the average media consumer has a limited attention span. Do you think your attention span decreases when you watch TV? Why or why not?

3. Can you think of an example from your everyday life when communication broke down because you didn't know something about your audience (receiver)?

4. Do you change the way you communicate (encode messages) when you're speaking to someone older than you? Younger than you? Why or why not?

5. Discuss the idea of feedback. What feedback does the president get when s/he gives a speech on TV? When you're talking to your friend? When an advertiser makes a commercial for a product? When a singer performs on stage?

ACTIVITY 21 **Evaluating roles in group discussions**

Think about your participation in the group discussion in this chapter. Go back to Activity 22 in Chapter 1 and answer the questions about your role on a separate sheet of paper or in an e-mail message to your instructor.

ACTIVITY 22 **Contacting college instructors by phone**

Sometimes it is necessary for you to contact your college instructors by phone if you are going to be absent, if you need to clarify an assignment, if you need to set up an office hour appointment, etc. Read through the information in the box that follows about leaving e-mail and phone messages for instructors.

STRATEGY

Learning Helpful Phone Message Hints

Using the phone to contact your instructors will be necessary at one point or another in your academic career. It is very important to be brief and direct, but also polite, during this contact. When you call your instructor, you are the "source" and your instructor is the "receiver"/ "destination," but you cannot rely on nonverbal factors to help you. Here are some other helpful hints:

- Remember to include your full name and any nickname you use in class (at the beginning of the message).
- State the name of the class and the day/hour it takes place; your instructor might have more than one section of the same course (at the beginning of the message).
- Keep the message brief; s/he might have several dozen messages to read or listen to daily.
- Make sure that your reason for missing class is a good one!
- Do not provide too much personal information. If your instructor wants more information from you, s/he will ask.
- Take responsibility for your own actions! If you have to miss class or receive a low grade on a test, don't blame anyone except yourself.
- Use polite phrases such as "I'll wait to hear from you" or "Thank you for your time."
- Do not flatter your instructor to try to get something you want.
- Tell your instructor how s/he can get in touch with you.
- If you need an appointment, offer several different times in order to accommodate your instructor's schedule.

ACTIVITY 23 **Recognizing appropriate language**

Read through the phone messages that were left by students. With a partner, analyze each message based on the criteria above. Discuss any strengths, weaknesses, and possible improvements for each message.

Phone Messages

1. "Hello Ms. Delk. This is Kim from your Tuesday/Thursday oral communication course. I won't be able to come to class today. I drank too much coffee last night and did not sleep well."

Strengths:

Weaknesses:

2. "Hello, Professor Shaw. This is Frank Cortell from your Wednesday morning speech class. I wanted to let you know that I need to leave class early this week—about 30 minutes—because I have a job interview on the other side of town. I'll be sure to sit near the door and get the homework from a classmate before next class. Thanks Professor."

Strengths:

Weaknesses:

3. "Hello this is Stephanie Brooks. Our final essay's due Friday, so I decided to ask you for help. I thought that showing my essay to you and getting some comments from you would be a good idea. Please let me have some of your time either today after 6 o'clock or tomorrow morning until 12 o'clock because my boyfriend's birthday is tomorrow, so I MUST go see him. Call me."

Strengths:

Weaknesses:

Part 3

ASSESSING YOUR LISTENING AND SPEAKING SKILLS

At the end of each chapter, you will find some tasks that will help you and your instructor evaluate whether you have learned the skills presented in the chapter. In addition, you will find some activities that ask you to reflect on your own progress.

ACTIVITY 24 Taking notes using a graphic organizer

Listen to a short section of a lecture about the role of feedback in interpersonal and mass communication. Take notes on a separate sheet of paper to give to your instructor. Use a graphic organizer in your notes. Focus on writing down the content words only.

ACTIVITY 25 Responding to short essay questions

Your instructor will choose questions from those the groups predicted in Activity 19. Answer the questions on a separate sheet of paper either in class or for homework.

ACTIVITY 26 Identifying syllables and stress patterns

The following words were either included in this chapter, in the reading or lecture, or may be otherwise related to the topic. Identify the stress patterns based on the general rules presented in Chapter 2.

1. distribution   [___ - ___]

2. identical   [___ - ___]

3. accurate   [___ - ___]

4. individual   [___ - ___]

5. minimize   [___ - ___]

6. incompatibility   [___ - ___]

ACTIVITY 27   Applying information from a lecture

Depending on your instructor's instructions, imagine you are in one of the following situations. Leave a voicemail message. Remember to identify who you are, which class you are in, why you are calling, and any other information you think is important.

- **a.** You're going to be absent from class on Friday
- **b.** You're going to be about a half hour late to the next class
- **c.** You want to know if you can make an appointment during the instructor's office hours to talk about your next presentation
- **d.** You would like the instructor to bring an extra copy of a handout you lost

After you complete the voicemail message, write answers to the following questions or discuss them with a classmate:

1. Did you think leaving a phone message was difficult? Why or why not?

_____

_____

2. Did you "practice" your message before you called? Why or why not?

_____

_____

3. Do you think your message was effective? Why or why not?

_____

_____

4. If you could do this assignment again, what changes would you make?

_____

_____

ACTIVITY 28 **Evaluating your progress**

Listed below are the objectives that were presented at the beginning of the chapter. Read through each one carefully, and evaluate your progress by checking: "Definitely need more help!", "Need a bit more practice!" or "Got it!"

Objectives	Definitely need more help!	Need a bit more practice!	Got it!
Recognize and use signal words of comparison			
Use symbols to note keywords			
Recognize syllable stress patterns in academic words			
Predict reading focus from diagrams and text			
Use signal words of comparison to include graphic organizers in notes			
Use notes to create concept cards			
Predict short essay exam questions and write effective answers			
Practice working in productive study groups			
Present oral summary of lecture notes			
Leave effective voicemail messages for your instructors			

WEB POWER

You will find additional exercises related to the content in this chapter at http://elt.thomson.com/collegeoral.

Do We Watch TV for Free?

ACADEMIC FOCUS:
BUSINESS ▶ TELEVISION ADVERTISING

Academic Listening and Speaking Objectives

In this chapter, you will continue to develop your skills as an academic listener and speaker. You will work individually, in pairs, and in small groups to:

- Develop vocabulary and expressions to discuss TV advertising
- Interpret graphs and tables related to upcoming lectures
- Recognize signal words of classification used in lectures
- Identify referent words to help understand lecture content
- Pronounce key vocabulary word forms with proper syllables, primary, and secondary stress
- Summarize lecture content and relate it to personal TV viewing habits
- Work in groups in different roles to discuss topics related to lectures
- Present information from a chart or table to classmates

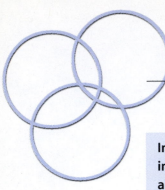

Part 1

EFFECTIVE ACADEMIC LISTENING

In this chapter, you will learn some of the language skills that are important in a business or advertising course. You will hear a lecture about television commercials and their costs. As you learn about this topic, you will continue participating in listening, note-taking, and speaking activities.

○ Getting Ready for the Lecture

As mentioned in earlier chapters, many instructors present material in lectures that is similar or related to information found in your textbooks. Textbooks often use tables and charts for factual information to support their statements. Instructors may refer to this information in their lectures, so understanding tables/charts beforehand will help you learn the material.

Interpreting Information in a Table or Chart

Charts and tables usually give numerical information. A chart uses circles, lines, and bars to present the information. A table is less visual. Instead of circles, lines, or bars, it usually has lists of numbers. When looking at a table or chart, you should follow these guidelines:

- Look at the title/heading/caption to see what is being presented and/or compared

- Determine what the numbers represent:
  - Percentages of something?
  - Units? (10 thousand, 10 million, or 10 billion)
  - Number of people?
  - Dollars? (spent, earned, etc.)
  - Ages?
  - Time?

- Compare the numbers in the table:
  - Is there a big difference between them?
  - What is the highest number?
  - What is the lowest?
  - What is the reason for the differences/similarities?

- Think about what the numbers mean:
  - What are possible explanations for the differences?
  - Who might be interested in using the information to support an argument?
  - What does this information imply?

ACTIVITY 1   Preparing for the content of a lecture

Look at the following charts and tables of information about the television industry and advertising. Use the guidelines in the previous box to make sure you understand the information.

A.

	TV Household Estimates Designated Market Area (DMA)—Ranked by Households Top Ten (of 211)		
Rank	**Designated Market Area (DMA)**	**TV Households**	**% of U.S.**
1	New York	7,376,330	6.80
2	Los Angeles	5,402,260	4.98
3	Chicago	3,399,460	3.14
4	Philadelphia	2,874,330	2.65
5	San Francisco-Oakland-San Jose	2,440,920	2.25
6	Boston (Manchester)	2,391,830	2.21
7	Dallas-Fort Worth	2,255,970	2.08
8	Washington D.C. (Hagstown)	2,224,070	2.05
9	Atlanta	2,035,060	1.88
10	Detroit	1,923,230	1.77
Nielsen Station Index (NSI)			

Source: http://www.nielsenmedia.com Reprinted by permission of Nielsen Media Research.

B.

Top U.S. Advertising Media by Revenue

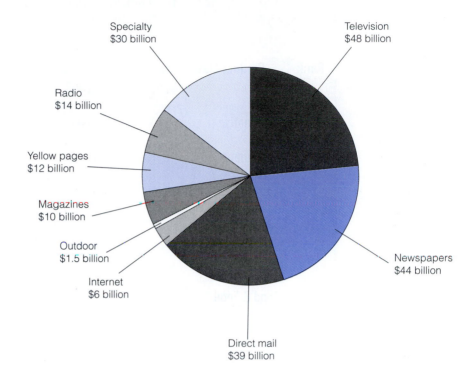

ADAPTED Statistical Abstract of the US, 1999, cited in Making Sense of the Media (Rodman, 2001, Pearson Education, p. 321). Internet adjusted for industry estimates.

C.

2003 TV Ad Revenue Figures Top 10 Local Broadcast TV Categories* Top 100 Markets First Half, 2003				
Rank	Product Classification	First Half 2003	First Half 2002	% Change
1	Automotive	$1,704,005.6	1,668,551.1	2.1
2	Restaurants	624,528.0	678,705.4	-8.0
3	Car & Truck Dealers	418,396.8	397,168.5	5.3
4	Telecommunications	338,605.3	334,082.2	1.4
5	Furniture Stores	302,631.0	287,602.3	5.2
6	Food & Food Products	270,866.7	257,115.7	5.3
7	Travel, Hotels, & Resorts	238,176.1	273,975.3	-13.1
8	Financial	224,219.4	219,273.3	2.3
9	Leisure Time Activities & Events	212,565.2	196,198.9	8.3
10	Insurance & Real Estate	188,502.6	194,489.0	-3.1

*Includes both local and national spot activity in the top 100 markets.

Source: Television Bureau of Advertising (TVB) from estimates supplied by TNS Media Intelligence/CMR.

D.

MAGNA Global Median Age Report Primetime Regular Series Median Age Trends (October–May) (Base = Persons 2+)					
	1998/99	1999/00	2000/01	2001/02	2002/03
ABC	41.8	43.4	46.6	46.0	43.6
CBS	53.1	52.4	51.2	51.7	52.2
NBC	43.4	45.2	45.1	45.9	46.2
FOX	34.0	35.2	36.0	36.0	35.0
UPN	37.4	32.8	34.1	34.2	33.1
WB	26.8	28.7	29.1	31.2	31.1
6-net average	43.3	44.1	44.8	44.9	44.7
U.S. Pop in TV HH	36.2	36.5	36.8	37.0	36.5

Source: MAGNA Global USA analysis of copyrighted Nielsen Media Research data. Reprinted by permission of Nielsen Media Research and with permission from Jack Myers Report.

ACTIVITY **2** **Understanding tables and charts**

Answer the following questions based on the charts and tables (labeled A, B, C, and D) from the previous pages.

1. Which table gives the number of TV viewers in major U.S. cities? Why do you think there are more cities in the top ten on the East Coast than on the West Coast?
2. Which table would you use to determine which network attracted the oldest viewers?
3. Which table could you use to find out how much money local broadcast TV channels made from advertisements about upcoming movies?
4. Which TV channel has consistently had the youngest viewers during primetime since 1998?
5. Which medium generated about $14 billion in advertising revenue in 1999?
6. Why do you think newspapers generate more advertising revenue than magazines do?
7. Do you think the Internet will make more or less money through advertising in the near future? Why?

STRATEGY

Pronouncing Numbers

In many lectures, you will hear numbers that describe amounts. You need to know how to write these amounts when you take notes and how to say these amounts when you are describing a chart or table.

942	Nine hundred and forty-two or nine hundred forty-two
9,420	Nine thousand four hundred and twenty or nine thousand four hundred twenty
90,420	Ninety thousand four hundred and twenty or ninety thousand four hundred twenty
904,200	Nine hundred and four thousand two hundred
2.2 million	Two point two million
2,245,890	Two million, two hundred and forty-five thousand, eight hundred and ninety or two million, two hundred forty-five thousand, eight hundred ninety
17%	Seventeen percent
17.5%	Seventeen point five percent
46 (age)	Forty-six years old
56 yrs.	Fifty-six years

ACTIVITY 3 **Recognizing and pronouncing numbers**

Sit with a partner and take turns answering the following questions aloud with the information from the tables and charts in Activity 1.

Student A: How many estimated TV households did Detroit have in 2002–03? (Table A)

Student B: *(1,899,901)*—One million eight hundred ninety-nine thousand nine hundred one.

1. How much money did furniture stores spend in the first half of 2003 on local broadcast TV commercials? (Table C)
2. What was the average age of WB viewers in 2002/2003? (Table D)
3. How many estimated TV households did Boston have in 2003–04? (Table A)
4. How much money did local broadcast TV make from restaurants who advertised on local and national commercials during the first half of 2003? (Table C)
5. How much was spent on outdoor advertising in 1999? (Chart B)
6. Approximately what percentage of TV households do the three largest cities in the United States make up? (Table A)

STRATEGY

Guessing Meaning from Context

Sometimes when you listen to a lecture, you will not always understand the vocabulary that the speaker uses, so you need to make intelligent guesses about the meanings of new words. You can:

- use the context, or language around the word
- use nonverbal cues the speaker provides
- use cognates, or words that are similar in other languages (e.g. "intermediate" in English and "intermedio" in Spanish)
- think about the grammatical use of the word

For example, if you heard the following in the lecture, could you guess what "initiate" means?

> The company recently built a new workout room in the basement of the building; therefore, many of the managers would like to initiate a new program to encourage employees to start exercising during lunch.

- "to initiate" indicates that it's a verb
- "new" gives us the idea that it's the beginning of something
initiate = start

ACTIVITY **4**   **Guessing meaning from context**

Lecturers may use words that are unfamiliar to all students in a lecture. These may be new academic words or words related to a particular field. Successful students who are listening actively pay close attention to the context of how the words are used and make intelligent guesses of their meanings. Listen to sentences from the lecture. Try to guess the meaning of each of the following words. Do not use your dictionary. The first one is done for you.

You will hear:

Spot advertising is when an advertiser purchases time from a specific station or a group of stations in a specific geographic area where they want a product ad to have more impact.

1. *Impact* probably means ___influence on people_____

2. *Options* probably means _____

3. *Segments* probably means _____

4a. *Assessed* probably means _____

4b. *Expenses* probably means _____

5. *Negotiated* probably means _____

6. *Cooperative* probably means _____

7. *Disposable* probably means _____

8. *Comprise* probably means _____

ACTIVITY 5 **Identifying stress patterns in academic words**

Look back at the information about syllable stress patterns in Chapter 2. Predict the stress patterns of the following words based on the part of speech, suffix, and/or number of syllables.

1. dispose   [___ - ___]

2. advertise   [___ - ___]

3. strategic   [___ - ___]

4. popularity   [___ - ___]

5. cooperate   [___ - ___]

6. cooperation   [___ - ___]

7. conserve   [___ - ___]

8. conservation   [___ - ___]

9. negotiate   [___ - ___]

10. option   [___ - ___]

11. comprise   [___ - ___]

12. estimate   [___ - ___]

STRATEGY

Recognizing Secondary Stress

In addition to primary stress on words, many longer words also have an additional stress that we often refer to as "secondary stress." This stress has a lower tone and is not as strong as the primary stress.

In a word like "rely," the stress changes based on the form of the word. In the noun form of the adjective "reliable," you should be able to recognize a secondary stress. The primary stress is on the fouth syllable, but there is also a secondary stress on the second syllable. We can indicate this secondary stress with a third number in our syllable stress numbering system.

re•ly′   [2-2]

re•li′•a•ble   [4-2]

re•li′•a•bi′•li•ty   [6-4-2] ("2" represents the secondary stress on the second syllable)

ACTIVITY **6**   **Recognizing secondary stress patterns**

Listen to the pronunciation of these words. Use the numbering system to indicate the number of syllables, primary stress, and secondary stress.

1. profitablitity   [_6_ - _4_ - _1_]

2. negotiation   [___ - ___ - ___]

3. geographic   [___ - ___ - ___]

4. similarity   [___ - ___ - ___]

5. recognition   [___ - ___ - ___]

6. estimation   [___ - ___ - ___]

7. disposability   [___ - ___ - ___]

8. popularity   [___ - ___ - ___]

○ Getting Information from the Lecture

The lecture you will hear is about the different types of television commercial costs based on different types of TV programs. You might hear a lecture like this in an advertising, marketing, or media course.

POWER GRAMMAR

Recognizing Words that Signal Classification

In previous chapters, we talked about signal words of:

- chronology (prior, until, at the end of the twentieth century, etc.)
- process (next, afterwards, let's turn to, finally, etc.)
- comparison-contrast (likewise, in contrast, unlike, etc.)

In the upcoming lecture, you will hear signal words of classification. Remember—recognizing signal words prepares you for what to listen for and helps you become a better listener and note-taker.

What you will hear

There are three types/kinds/<u>categories</u> of . . .

<u>Three types/kinds/categories</u> of X are . . .

<u>Several/Some types</u> of X are . . .

X can be divided into <u>three parts</u>

X consists of <u>three types</u>

X comprises <u>three segments</u>

X, Y, and Z are <u>kinds of/types of</u>/etc.

What you should expect/do

You should immediately make some sort of list that you can "fill in as you go." Even if you don't hear all the items right away, at least start making a list using classification markers such as numbers, letters, or bullets.

1.	a.	•
2.	b.	•
3.	c.	•

ACTIVITY 7 **Organizing with signal words of classification**

Listen to the following excerpts from the lecture. Listen for the signal words of classification and take notes on the information using classification markers as well as abbreviations and symbols.

You will hear:

Today I want to answer a few questions that you might have about television advertising. Uh, for example, what is the main goal of television commercials? How are they structured? And, with all the channels available on broadcast and cable TV today, what are the different options available to advertisers?

> **Master Student Tip**
>
> You should leave extra room in your list to add definitions, additional information, examples, etc.

You should write in your notes:

TV Adv. ?s

a. Main goal

b. Structure

c. Diff. avail. options

1.

2.

3.

4.

POWER GRAMMAR

Recognizing Reference Words/Expressions in Lectures

Speakers often use reference words/expressions in their lectures to refer back to something previously said. For example, imagine someone saying the following:

> Among the five <u>types of television advertising</u>, the <u>second type of television advertising</u> is much less broad. This <u>second type of advertising</u> is called spot advertising. This <u>second type of advertising</u>, called spot advertising, is when an advertiser purchases time from a specific station in a specific geographic area.

Doesn't the sentence sound funny? Isn't it repetitive?
> *Instead, a lecturer would probably say:*

> Among the <u>five types of television advertising</u>, the <u>second</u> is much less broad. This <u>one</u> is called spot advertising. <u>This is when</u> an advertiser purchases time from a specific station in a specific geographic area.

Types of Reference Words

Pronouns: it, this, that, these, those, s/he, here, there, they, them, etc.

Substitution: one, ones, each, first, second, last, etc. (leaving out part of a noun phrase instead of repeating it) (There are <u>six major TV networks</u> ... the <u>first</u> is) first = major TV network

ACTIVITY 8 Recognizing reference strategies in lectures

Listen to the following sentences from the lecture and identify what the following reference strategies refer to.

You will hear:

> Local advertising is based on the city or community. <u>It</u> includes ad time bought on either local stations or cable stations by local businesses.

1. It = *local advertising* _____

2. they = _____

3. it = _____

4. these = _____

5. this = _____

6. the first, the second, the last = _____

ACTIVITY 9 Connecting ideas to the lecture

The following sentences are based on information from the lecture you will hear. Predict whether you think the sentences are "true" (T) or "false" (F). After the lecture, come back to these sentences and make any corrections using your lecture notes.

1. T / F   Most commercials are usually 60 seconds long.

2. T / F   About 10 percent of TV programming is made up of commercials.

3. T / F   Commercials during the TV program, *Friends*, were the most expensive.

4. T / F   Commercials for local companies are the most popular and usually shown during prime time.

5. T / F   "Spot ads" are used by advertisers to focus on a particular city or region.

6. T / F   TV viewers between 18–34 years old do not spend as much money as other age groups.

ACTIVITY 10 Taking complete notes

This lecture focuses on the different types of commercials on television. The lecture is divided into sections. Your instructor will decide how many parts of the lecture to work with before you stop to review your notes.

Questions/Comments	Notes
What are the different goals of TV advertising?	Goals of TV industry: Non-Program material: Five categories of TV Commercials: A. • Length of commercials B.

Questions/Comments (cont.)	Notes
	C.
	D.
	E.

STRATEGY

Understanding Oral Instructions for Class Assignments

Some instructions for assignments in academic courses are written in the syllabus or course description that you receive at the beginning of the course. You also might receive written assignments during the semester. However, instructors also give information about assignments orally in class, often at the end of a lecture. This information usually contains important details about an assignment:

- what resources you need to use
- what you need to do (be careful—there may be more than one part of the assignment)
- when it is due
- how it needs to be done (e.g. orally, written, length, etc.)

Don't interrupt the instructor until you are certain s/he is finished describing the assignment. Students are often too concerned with the due date and length and may miss other important details.

ACTIVITY **11** **Taking notes on homework**

Listen to the description of the homework assignment and take careful notes about what you need to do, when the assignment is due, and how the instructor wants it to be done.

Homework Assignment:

_____

_____

_____

_____

_____

_____

_____

_____

○ Making Your Notes Useful

ACTIVITY 12 Summarizing and paraphrasing content

Successful students benefit the most from a lecture by thinking and talking about it shortly after listening to it. Follow these guidelines to help you remember information from the lecture.

1. Take five minutes to look over your notes.
2. Put your notes away and write down (paraphrase) as many of the lecture's main ideas as you can remember.
3. Sit with a partner and *without looking at your original notes or main ideas*, talk about the information you remember. Make sure you cover the following:
   a. Goals of TV Industry
   b. Types of Non-Program Material
   c. Length of Commercials
   d. Types of Commercials
4. Check your original notes/paraphrased information only if necessary.

ACTIVITY 13 Confirming information about homework

Review Activity 11 when you took notes about the homework assignment your instructor described. Answer the following questions.

1. What do you need to do first to start the assignment?
2. What type of program do you need to watch?
3. What other information about the program do you need?
4. What are the four categories of non-program material you need to watch for?
5. What are the three target audiences the instructor mentioned?
6. How long does the report need to be?
7. Does it have to be typed?
8. What other questions do you have about the assignment?

Part 2

EFFECTIVE ACADEMIC SPEAKING

In speaking about academic topics, both students and instructors sometimes refer to hypothetical situations to better understand the content. Since advertising surrounds us, it is usually not difficult to think about how it directly affects us.

ACTIVITY 14 **Discussing topics related to the lecture**

Review the guidelines from Chapter 1 about working in groups and the expressions for stating opinions, agreeing, and disagreeing. Assign yourselves different roles: leader, reporter, or participant, and discuss the questions on the next page.

Assignments:

Leader: _____

Reporter: _____

Participant: _____

Participant: _____

LIFE WITHOUT ADVERTISING

Advertising is often portrayed as a negative force in media. Is that true? Imagine your life without any advertising of any kind. No more interruptions in your favorite television show. No distracting billboards along the highway. No pictures of food or clothing interspersed with your daily news. No sample perfumes falling out of your magazine. No pesky direct mail pieces in your mailbox.

1. What strategies would you have to use to get the information previously provided by advertising? How would you learn about new products?
2. How would you know when your favorite music group is appearing in your area?
3. How would you learn about political candidates?
4. What would you do to get comparative information on a CD player or camera?
5. How would you know which department store carries the clothing you need?
6. How would you know which grocery store has the best prices on soft drinks this week?
7. What would you do to get the information you need to make purchasing decisions?
8. "The only purpose for TV is to deliver its audiences to advertisers." Do you agree or disagree with this statement? Why?

Reprinted by permission of the Newspaper Association of America Foundation.

ACTIVITY 15 **Evaluating your role in group discussions**

Think about your participation in the group discussion in this chapter. Write the answers to the questions from Activity 21 in Chapter 1 on a separate sheet of paper or in an e-mail message to your instructor.

STRATEGY

Describing a Chart/Table

Interpreting data in a chart or table out loud to another person or group of people is good speaking practice. You need to:

- state the subject of the chart or table
- present the information in an organized, meaningful way based on the chart or graph's visual layout (e.g. top to bottom, left to right, clockwise)
- pronounce numbers clearly (look back at Activity 2)
- describe the pattern
- present possible interpretation, predictions, or results of the pattern

Possible Expressions to Use

"The subject of this table is _____."

"The information is presented in descending/ascending/alphabetical/ etc. order." (general description of the content of the rows)

"The first/middle/last/etc. column shows/represents _____."

"This table shows us (that) _____."

"It is possible that in the future, _____."

ACTIVITY 16 **Explaining a chart or graph**

Form small groups. Review the steps in the preceding box, "Describing a Chart/Table." Go back to the tables and chart from Activity 1 in this chapter. Each group member is responsible for describing the information from one of these examples out loud to the other members. Members should make sure that each speaker:

- States the subject/purpose
- Presents the information in an organized, meaningful way
- Explains the pattern
- Provides a possible interpretation

Example:

Top Ten Primetime Broadcast TV Programs for week of 9/22/03–9/28/03			
Rank	**Program**	**Network**	**Total Viewers**
1	CSI	CBS	26,907,000
2	Friends	NBC	24,539,000
3	E.R.	NBC	23,223,000
4	Will & Grace	NBC	20,286,000
5	Everybody Loves Raymond	CBS	20,628,000
6	Law and Order	NBC	20,861,000
7	Two and a Half Men	CBS	18,441,000
8	Survivor: Pearl Islands	CBS	19,864,000
9	CSI: Miami	CBS	17,396,000
10	NFL Monday Night Football	ABC	17,301,000

Slightly adapted from http://www.nielsenmedia.com. Reprinted by permission of Nielsen Media Research.

> **Master Student Tip**
>
> Explain any words you think your audience may not know; write them on the board or overhead transparency.

Description (Example): The subject of this table is the ranking of prime-time shows based on the number of viewers during the week of September 22 to 28, 2003. The information is presented in descending order with the highest ranked show listed first. The far left-hand column represents the TV show; the middle column gives the network of the show; the last column shows the number of viewers. This table shows us that CBS is currently the most popular network during primetime with five of its programs making the top ten list. It also proves the popularity of CBS's programs "CSI" with more than 44 million viewers tuning in to its two shows—CSI and CSI Miami. However, NBC holds four of the top five shows with almost 70 million viewers. The table also shows the continued popularity of reality television shows like 'Survivor.' It is possible that in the future, other networks will take the lead as the popularity of TV programs decrease and increase.

Part 3

At the end of each chapter, you will find some tasks that will help you and your instructor evaluate whether you have learned the skills presented in the chapter. In addition, you will find some activities that ask you to reflect on your own progress.

 ACTIVITY **17** **Getting complete assignments**

Listen to the following descriptions of assignments given during a class. As you listen, take notes so that you remember the important parts of the assignment. When you are finished, answer the true-false questions for each one.

1.

True or False?

a. ____ The name of the article is "We Don't Need TV."

b. ____ The article is about eight pages long.

c. ____ You can find the article on the instructor's website.

d. ____ You need to send five questions to the instructor by e-mail.

2.

True or False?

a. ____ The instructor has office hours on Monday mornings.

b. ____ The paper needs to be less than five pages.

c. ____ You can find information for the paper in the syllabus.

d. ____ The topic of the paper concerns your personal TV viewing habits.

ACTIVITY 18 Presenting information from a chart or table

Go to the Thomson Heinle website for this chapter and explore the information from media websites. Choose a chart or table that interests you to explain to the whole class. Refer to Activity 16 for guidelines on presenting data from a chart or table.

○ Assessing Your Speaking

Your instructor may use this checklist to evaluate your use of academic English in your speaking assignments.

Presenting a chart or table	OK	Needs work	Example(s)
Content:			
• stated subject of table or chart clearly			
• provided a possible interpretation of the information			
Organization:			
• explained how the information is presented			
• explained the pattern in the table			
• used classification structures when appropriate			
Pronunciation:			
• used syllable stress appropriately on academic words			
• pronounces final -s endings when appropriate			

Reflecting on what you have learned

Complete the following sentences based on the material and activities from this chapter.

1. Some words I learned about TV advertising that I didn't know before are . . .

2. Secondary stress is different from primary stress in that . . .

3. Two common signal words/expressions of classification are . . .

4. When an instructor uses a signal word for classification during a lecture, I should . . .

5. One type of reference word that lecturers use is . . .

6. When an instructor gives instructions for an assignment, I should . . .

7. When presenting information from a table, I need to . . .

8. One new note-taking technique I learned is to . . .

ACTIVITY 20 **Evaluating your progress**

Listed on the next page are the objectives that were presented at the beginning of the chapter. Read through each one carefully, and evaluate your progress by checking: "Definitely need more help!", "Need a bit more practice!" or "Got it!"

Objectives	Definitely need more help!	Need a bit more practice!	Got it!
Develop vocabulary and expressions to discuss TV advertising			
Interpret graphs and tables related to upcoming lectures			
Recognize signal words of classification used in lectures			
Identify referent words to help understand lecture content			
Pronounce key vocabulary word forms with proper syllables, primary stress, and secondary stress			
Summarize lecture content and relate it to personal TV viewing habits			
Work in groups in different roles to discuss topics related to lectures			
Present information from a chart or table to classmates			

WEB POWER

You will find additional exercises related to the content in this chapter at **http://elt.thomson.com/collegeoral**.

Does Violence in the Media Make Us Violent?

ACADEMIC FOCUS:
SOCIAL PSYCHOLOGY ▶ MEDIA EFFECTS

Academic Listening and Speaking Objectives

In this chapter, you will continue to develop your skills as an academic listener and speaker. You will work individually, in pairs, and in small groups to:

- Learn word forms, syllable stress patterns, and meanings of academic words in context
- Recognize points of view in readings and lectures
- Identify and use contrastive stress
- Use signal words of cause and effect to aid in note-taking
- Take lecture notes on a controversial topic
- Identify facts and opinions
- Demonstrate active listening and questioning skills in discussions
- Express opinions using academically appropriate language
- Use information from course material to support an opinion

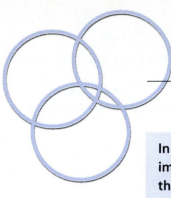

Part 1

EFFECTIVE ACADEMIC LISTENING

In this chapter, you will learn some of the language skills that are important in a social psychology course. You will hear a lecture about the effects of media violence and participate in listening, note-taking, and speaking activities related to this highly debatable topic.

○ Getting Ready for the Lecture

ACTIVITY **1** **Preparing for a lecture's content**

With a partner, discuss which of the following statements you agree with and why. Compare your opinions with two other students.

1. An action movie would not be interesting without violence.

2. The government should control the content of television programs.

3. Playing video games helps relieve tension.

4. Violence in the news is much different from violence in movies.

5. Violent lyrics in gangsta rap music cause men to be disrespectful to women.

6. Teenagers should be able to buy any video game they want.

7. Young children are more affected by violence in the media than adults are.

8. Watching violence on TV makes people think the world is a bad place.

ACTIVITY 2   Using context to learn meanings of new words

The words that follow are found in the first reading and perhaps in the lecture you will hear. Figure out the meanings of the underlined words using their context. Choose the correct definition from the list.

a. design, make

b. almost but not quite, nearly

c. act with each other

d. to misinterpret, misconstrue

e. to observe in detail

f. concentrated on

g. brought to an end

h. unprotected

1. _____ Researchers believe it is important to underline{investigate} the potential effects of playing violent video games.

2. _____ Computer animators underline{create} the characters and scenes found in video games.

3. _____ The news on every channel underline{focused} on the hurricane that occurred this morning.

4. _____ It is important that news reporters not underline{distort} any facts of a story when they are writing an article; the readers expect the truth.

5. _____ I was surrounded by trees that were so tall and thick with leaves that the sun was underline{virtually} blocked out.

6. _____ Long-term underline{exposure} to the sun without sunscreen protection causes wrinkles, especially on the delicate skin of the face.

7. _____ After the speaker underline{concluded} her presentation, she asked if there were any further questions.

8. _____ Salespeople must have excellent communication skills; they underline{interact} with many people on the phone and in person every day.

ACTIVITY 3 **Learning stress patterns**

The words that follow are important in the reading and lecture you will hear. Some of them may be new to you. Be prepared to pronounce them correctly. Use the numbering system you learned in Chapter 1.

1. create [___ - ___]

2. investigate [___ - ___]

3. focus [___ - ___]

4. target [___ - ___]

5. issue [___ - ___]

6. illogical [___ - ___]

7. constant [___ - ___]

8. consequence [___ - ___]

9. distortion [___ - ___]

10. virtual [___ - ___]

11. exposure [___ - ___]

12. conclusion [___ - ___]

13. interactive [___ - ___]

14. participant [___ - ___]

15. majority [___ - ___]

16. exceed [___ - ___]

ACTIVITY **4** **Finding word forms in the dictionary**

With a partner, see if you can answer the questions that follow. If neither of you knows the answer, look up the other forms in an English-English dictionary. Predict the syllable stress pattern using the patterns you studied in Chapter 2 or, if necessary, use a dictionary to help you. The first one is done for you.

Word forms	Syllable stress
1. *Distortion* is a noun. What's the verb? _distort_	[_2_ - _2_]
2. *Constant* is an adjective. What's the adverb? _____	[__ - __]
3. *Exposure* is a noun. What's the verb? _____	[__ - __]
4. *Conclusion* is a noun. What's the verb? _____	[__ - __]
5. *Interactive* is an adjective. What's the verb? _____ What's the noun? _____	[__ - __] [__ - __]
6. *Virtual* is an adjective. What's the adverb? _____	[__ - __]
7. *Investigate* is a verb. What's the noun (thing)? _____ What's the noun (person)? _____	[__ - __] [__ - __]
8. *Create* is a verb. What's the noun (person)? _____ What's the noun (thing)? _____ What's the adjective? _____ What's the adverb? _____	[__ - __] [__ - __] [__ - __] [__ - __]

ACTIVITY **5** **Predicting the main idea of a reading**

Based on the article's title in Activity 6, do you think the author is "for" or "against" the video game industry?

_____

_____

_____

_____

_____

_____

_____

ACTIVITY **6** **Reading material to prepare for a lecture**

Read the following article to prepare you for the lecture on media violence and the short answer test.

GROUP CITES VIDEO-GAME MAKERS FOR VIOLENCE AGAINST WOMEN

WASHINGTON (AP) – A watchdog[1] group warned Thursday that video games are featuring increased violence against women and called on retailers to do a better job of keeping such games out of the hands of children.

The video game trade association called the report by the National Institute on Media and the Family "illogical and grotesquely unfair."

In its annual review of the video game industry, the Minneapolis-based institute singled out several games, most notably "Grand Theft Auto: Vice City." In that game, participants ramp up[2] their score by having sex with a prostitute, and gain additional points by killing her. The game includes scenes in which blood splatters out of a woman's body as the player beats her to death. Rep. Betty McCollum, D-Minn., said such games "are creating a culture of virtual victimizers."

The game is rated M for Mature audiences (over age 17), but children have no trouble buying it, said David Walsh, the institute's president and author of the report. The institute gave the industry an overall grade of F.

"Young children have no trouble getting these games," Walsh said. Sen. Joseph Lieberman, D-Conn., who has spearheaded[3] efforts to limit children's exposure to violence in the media, credited the industry for ceasing[4] to market their adult games to children.

But he said parents and retailers need to do more to prevent children from getting the violent games. The most troubling trend, Lieberman said, is that "women are the new targets of choice in the most violent games."

He said it might be time for a new round of congressional hearings.

Doug Lowenstein, president of the video game trade group, Interactive Digital Software Association, said the report's focus on violence against women was a distortion.

"They cite[5] one or two games where they have issues," he said. "This is an industry where the average age is 28."

He pointed to a Federal Trade Commission study issued in 2000 which found that adults were present for 82 percent of video game purchases.

As far as the violence in "Grand Theft Auto," Lowenstein said, "I won't get into individual creative elements of these games. The games are properly rated . . . You can't sanitize interests."

Dawn Berrie, a spokeswoman for Take-Two Interactive, which owns the manufacturer of Grand Theft Auto, said in a statement that "the company makes every effort to market its games responsibly, (and) target advertising and marketing only to adult consumers over the age of 17."

The report said only 70 percent of retailers have polices preventing children from buying or renting games rated M. That figure is slightly higher, 75 percent, for chain stores[6].

Hal Halpin, president of the Interactive Entertainment Merchants Association, a trade group for chain stores that sell video games, said the stores have improved over recent years.

"We're actively working to educate our own clerks at the store level as well as customers and parents," he said.

Frommer, Frederic J., "Group Cites Video-Game Makers for Violence Against Women," Associated Press, December 19, 2002. Reprinted with permission of The Associated Press.

1. *watchdog* = protector or guardian
2. *ramp up* = increase
3. *spearhead* = to lead
4. *ceasing* = stopping
5. *cite* = show as an example
6. *chain stores* = stores under same ownership

ACTIVITY 7 **Scanning a text for specific information**

Look back at the article and identify the occupation of each person mentioned.

1. _____ Hal Halpin

2. _____ Doug Lowenstein

3. _____ David Walsh

4. _____ Dawn Berrie

5. _____ Betty McCollum

6. _____ Joseph Lieberman

a. President, Interactive Digital Software Association

b. Spokesperson, Take Two Interactive, makers of Grand Theft Auto

c. Democratic Senator from Connecticut

d. President, Interactive Entertainment Merchants Association

e. Democratic Congressperson from Minnesota

f. President, National Institute on Media and the Family

g. Creator of Grand Theft Auto

ACTIVITY 8 **Identifying different points of view in a reading**

The following people stated opinions in the previous article. Determine whether each person supports the video game industry or opposes it based on her/his job title/occupation and comments. Put each person's name in the appropriate column.

Hal Halpin Dawn Berrie
Doug Lowenstein Joseph Lieberman
David Walsh Betty McCollum

Supporting the video game industry	Opposing the video game industry

STRATEGY

Identifying Contrastive Stress

In Chapter 3, you learned that content words are usually stressed in sentences, and function words are usually reduced. In a single sentence, there is usually one content word (one syllable) that receives the strongest stress in the sentence. This is usually the final content word of the sentence, and we call this the "focal stress."

For example:

> <u>Young</u> <u>children</u> <u>have</u> <u>no</u> <u>trouble</u> <u>getting</u> this <u>video</u> GAME.

All the content words (young, children, have, no, trouble, getting, games) receive syllable stress, but "game" receives the focal stress (main stress) of the entire sentence.

However, sometimes a speaker wants to emphasize a different word in the sentence:

- to express a strong opinion (usually disagreement)
- to clarify/correct something previously said

If the speaker uses contrastive stress, any word in the sentence can be stressed.

For example:

> <u>Young</u> <u>children</u> <u>have</u> <u>no</u> <u>trouble</u> getting THIS <u>video</u> <u>game</u>.

It is understood here that the speaker is singling out a particular video game by emphasizing the word "this" and perhaps holding up the game or pointing to its title or picture.

ACTIVITY 9 **Recognizing contrastive stress in responses**

Listen and read along with the students' questions about the article from Activity 6. Listen carefully to the instructor's responses and write down the missing word that contrasts with the students' questions.

Example:

Student: According to David Walsh, do children have trouble buying "Grand Theft Auto: Vice City"?

Instructor: Not at all. He said children have ___no___ trouble buying "Grand Theft Auto: Vice City."

1. Student: Is Doug Lowenstein a spokesperson for Interactive Digital Software Association?

   Instructor: No, Lowenstein is _____ of Interactive Digital Software Association.

2. Student: Does Hal Halpin say that chain stores have not improved in their sales of video games to children in recent years?

   Instructor: That's not accurate. He said chain stores _____ improved in their sales of video games to children in recent years.

3. Student: Did the article point out that 17 percent of retailers have policies preventing children from buying or renting M-rated video games?

   Instructor: No—almost the opposite—the article mentioned that _____ of retailers have policies preventing children from buying or renting M-rated video games.

4. Student: Did the spokesperson for "Grand Theft Auto" say that the company is making some effort to market its game responsibly?

   Instructor: The spokesperson for "Grand Theft Auto" says that the company is making _____ effort to market its game responsibly.

○ **Getting Information from the Lecture**

The lecture you will hear in this chapter is about the effects of media violence on viewers. You might hear a lecture like this in a sociology, psychology, or communications course.

P O W E R   G R A M M A R

Recognizing Words that Signal Cause and Effect

In previous chapters, you listened for different types of signal words. In this chapter, you will hear information about the effects of media violence. For example, you might hear in the lecture:

> Children may behave more aggressively <u>as a result</u> of watching increased amounts of media violence.

In this example, the cause is "watching increased amounts of media violence" and the effect is "may behave more aggressively." The speaker makes the connection between these two actions by using a common cause and effect expression: "as a result of."

Linking two clauses:	when, because, since
Linking a noun phrase + clause:	as a result of, because of
Linking two noun phrases:	cause(s), lead(s) to, contribute(s) to, result(s) in, produce(s), is/are more likely to
Transitions:	as a result, . . . therefore/consequently
Other expressions:	the more . . . the more . . .

A technique you can use to capture cause-effect ideas in your notes is to use the symbols $<$, $>$, $\rightarrow$, or $\leftarrow$.

> X $>$ Y (X causes Y)   or   X $\leftarrow$ Y (X is caused by Y)

Or a chain reaction:

> X $>$ Y $>$ Z (X leads to Y which results in Z)

In the following sentence, what is the cause and what is the effect?

> Media violence produces many unhealthy effects in children.
> media viol. $>$ unhealthy eff. childrn.

ACTIVITY **10**   **Recognizing signal words of cause and effect**

In each of the following sentences, underline the word(s) that signal cause and effect. Then, put a "C" above each cause and an "E" above each effect. The first one is done for you.

1. Children are exposed to more video violence than they were fifty years ago <u>because</u> they have video games, the Internet, more television channels, and movies.

2. Boys may learn to be disrespectful and abusive toward women because of what they see in the media.

3. Children's programming is a lot better than it used to be as a result of pressure from media and family organizations.

4. Households that use the V-chip are more likely to have better parental control over what children watch on TV.

5. Watching violence in action movies may lead to a release of aggression.

6. Technology such as the V-chip and software to block websites has developed quickly over the past decade. Consequently, parents can better control what comes into their own houses.

ACTIVITY **11** **Listening to signal words and taking notes**

Listen to the following sentences and take notes, writing down only the keywords and using symbols or strategies to show cause and effect.

You will hear:

Perhaps there were experiences of real violence in their childhood that led them to become more violent, not simply by watching violent cartoons on TV.

You should write:

Exp. real viol. as child > become more viol.

≠ watch'g viol. TV cartoons

1.

2.

3.

4.

5.

ACTIVITY 12 **Taking notes to get information**

Now you will listen to a lecture and take notes to help you remember what you heard and prepare for discussions and a test. The lecture is divided into three parts. Your instructor will decide how many parts of the lecture to work with before you stop to review your notes.

Part 1. Introduction

Questions/Comments	Notes

Part 2. Critics of media violence

Recall/Questions	Notes
	Argument #1 Argument #2 Argument #3 Argument #4

Transition to "Other" Side	

Part 3. Defenders of media

Recall/Questions	Notes
	Argument #1
	Argument #2
	Argument #3
	Argument #4

◯ Making Your Notes Useful

ACTIVITY 13 Identifying questions with a partner

Review your notes with a partner and fill in the "recall" column with questions/comments you would like to ask your instructor.

ACTIVITY 14 Identifying the main ideas of a lecture

Review your notes and underline the major arguments for each side. Read the sentences that follow and determine whether each one is an argument "opposing" (O) media violence or "defending" (D) the media.

1. _____ Young children learn aggressive behavior from television and film.

2. _____ Aggressive behavior has been around forever and has been portrayed in great literature. Today, the media are simply showing the stories that we instinctively enjoy seeing.

3. _____ The term "violence" is often not defined in a realistic way.

4. _____ Extensive exposure to media violence can cause desensitization.

5. _____ Children who constantly watch violent TV programs are more likely to act aggressively later in life than children who don't watch as much.

6. _____ Violence on TV doesn't cause violence in people; there are usually other factors involved.

7. _____ Watching violence in the media makes us think the world is a mean place.

8. _____ The media show our society as a violent place because it IS a violent place.

ACTIVITY 15 **Connecting other information to the lecture**

Work with a partner and decide to which argument from the lecture each of the following statements is related. Write the number or numbers of the argument from Activity 14 in the space provided. Discuss your opinions with your partner. The first one is done for you.

1. ___5___ "A study of population data for various countries showed homicide rates doubling within the 10 to 15 years after the introduction of television …"*

2. _____ "Television is an easy target for the concern about violence in our society but a misleading one. We should no longer waste time worrying about this subject. Instead let us turn our attention to the obvious major causes of violence, which include poverty, racial conflict, drug abuse, and poor parenting."†

3. _____ There is much confusion about the definition of "violence" and terms like "media violence" and "violent video games." Psychologists define violence and aggression as "the intentional injury of another person." However, there is neither intent to injure nor a living victim in a video game.‡

* Source: Centerwall, BS: Exposure to television as a cause of violence. In Comstock G (ed): Public Communication as Behavior. Orlando, Fla.: Academic Press Inc.; 1989, 2: 1–58.
† Source: Jonathan Freedman, Ph.D. Professor of Psychology, University of Toronto in The Harvard Mental Health Letter, May 1996.
‡ Source: "Does Playing Violent Video Games Cause Aggressive Behavior?" Paper given at the Cultural Policy Center, University of Chicago on October 27, 2001 by Jeffrey Goldstein, Ph.D., University of Utrecht, The Netherlands, http://culturalpolicy.uchicago.edu/conf2001/papers/goldstein.html.

4. _____ "Other researchers…investigated and confirmed that heavy [TV] viewers tend to be poor, uneducated, unemployed people who live in high-crime neighborhoods. Mean-world attitudes, as other studies have shown, correlate with personal experience with crime, not with TV-viewing."*

5. _____ "Throughout history, violence has been a matter of public fascination and absorption, as the Bible, the Iliad, and the works of Shakespeare attest. That today's media continue to reflect this enduring aspect of our culture is neither surprising nor a basis for condemnation."†

6. _____ "Due to their role-modeling capacity to promote real world violence, there is deep concern that playing violent video games, with their fully digitalized human images, will cause children to become more aggressive towards other children and become more tolerant of, and more likely to engage in, real-life violence."‡

---

*Source: Rhodes, R. The media violence myth. *Rolling Stone*, November 23, 2000.

†Source: American Booksellers Foundation for Free Expression, American Society of Journalists and Authors, Association of American Publishers, Inc., Association of American University Presses, Authors Guild, Freedom to Read Foundation, PEN American Center (Violence in the Media: A Joint Statement), http://www.abffe.com/mediaviolence.htm.

‡Source: Robert E. McAfee, M.D., Immediate Past President, American Medical Association, Testimony before House Energy and Commerce Committee Subcommittee on Telecommunications and Finance, June 1994.

Becoming a Critical Thinker and Listener

As college students and educated adults, we need to be critical thinkers and listeners. This means we should evaluate everything we hear before accepting or rejecting it. In order to evaluate information, we need to consider who says it (the source) and whether it is a fact or an opinion. Here are some other differences between facts and opinions:

Characteristics of Facts and Opinions

Facts (objective)	**Opinions (subjective)**
The statement is from someone who usually doesn't have a personal interest in the success (or failure) of something.	The statement is from someone who has a personal interest in the success (or failure) of something.
The statement is something generally accepted and considered true.	The statement is something accepted by some, but not by others.
The statement is something observable, measurable, and/or provable.	The statement usually reflects personal evaluation (good, bad) or emotion.

Examples

Fact:
A 1999 survey of 495 Rhode Island parents led by Judith Owens, a Brown University professor, found that children who have TVs in their bedrooms are more likely to suffer from sleep disturbances.
- Judith Owens seems to be an unbiased (objective) source
- Statement contains information from a survey (observable)

Opinion:
The government should decide whether certain TV violence is appropriate or not.
- Not everyone would agree with this opinion
- Statement seems to be based on a personal evaluation of TV

Source: September 27, 1999 Brown University News Service. "Television at bedtime is associated with sleep difficulties in children."

ACTIVITY 16 Listening for tone and point of view

Listen to the following statements from other researchers, writers, etc., about the media violence issue. Take brief notes on what you hear. Then circle whether you think the statement opposes media violence or defends it; also decide whether it's a fact or an opinion.

Master Student Tip

College instructors often have guest speakers or show video clips of other experts. This information is often related to the lecture topics— you should include it in your notes!

1.

Notes	
	opposing or defending
	fact or opinion

Source: Cited on the Kaiser Family Foundation website
http://www.kff.org/content/2002/3271/Video_Game_Key_Facts.pdf; original source is *Fair Play: Violence, Gender, and Race in Video Games* (Oakland, CA: Children Now), 2001.

2.

Notes	
	opposing or defending
	fact or opinion

Source: http://www.psych.org/public_info/media_violence.cfm

3.

Notes	
	opposing or defending
	fact or opinion

Source: Susan Fitzgerald, reporter for the *Philadelphia Inquirer*, March 29, 2002, www.philly.com.

4.

Notes	
	opposing or defending
	fact or opinion

Source: Dr. Leonard Eron, University of Illinois at Chicago, Testimony before the Senate Committee on Commerce, Science and Transportation, Subcommittee on Communications, June 12, 1995.

STRATEGY

Synthesizing Information

In all your classes, you will get information from different sources, mostly lectures, textbooks, and handouts. The information will be related in some way, and you need to figure out how it is related. In other words, you need to *synthesize* the information. To use this chapter as an example, you read information from various researchers about the role of violence in the media and you listened to a lecture about both "sides" of the issue.

ACTIVITY 17 Synthesizing information for writing

Answer the following question(s) on a separate sheet of paper. Save your response(s) for later discussion and activities.

After reading about violent video games, hearing a lecture presenting both sides of the argument, and hearing other "guest" lecturers, how do you feel about the issue? Of all the arguments that you have heard in favor of or against violence in the media, which one do you think is the strongest? Why?

Part 2

EFFECTIVE ACADEMIC SPEAKING

You may find it easy to disagree with your friends about what movie to go see, or who the best baseball team is, or whether you like a certain instructor. However, during a classroom discussion, it is important to express your opinion in academically acceptable ways *and* to provide reasons for your agreement and/or disagreement. During this chapter, you have listened to many facts and opinions about the causes and effects of media violence. The next step is to use what you have learned in discussions.

POWER GRAMMAR

Asking and Responding to Open and Closed Questions

There are different types of questions that can be used to stimulate discussion about a topic. It's important to be able to ask and answer these different types of questions. Closed questions usually only require a one-word response, but they can become more "open" if followed by another short question.

Example:

> Do you think young children learn how to fight from playing violent video games? In what ways?

> Instead of simply answering "yes," the student who answers also needs to give more information.

Question Words/Expressions for "Open" Questions

How …?	What …?	In what ways …?
Under what conditions …?	Give some examples.	Describe X.
Suppose …	What would happen if …?	Tell me/ Show me.
Do you think …? Why?	What do you think about …?	Why or why not?

ACTIVITY 18 Recognizing "open" questions

Look at the sample questions about violence on TV. Which of the questions are "closed" questions? Which are "open" questions? Underline the words/expressions that make the questions "open." The first one has been done for you.

Topic: Violence on TV reflecting violence in society

1. In what ways do you think the violence on TV reflects what is really going on in our society?
2. Do you think TV is too violent?
3. If there were no violence on TV, do you think real violence would decrease? Why or why not?
4. What real events do you know about that you think were based on something in the media?
5. What is the most violent movie you have ever seen on TV?

ACTIVITY 19 Writing questions for group discussions

Your instructor will assign your group one of the following topics. With your group, prepare three (3) questions that will stimulate discussion. Use the information about questions from the previous activities.

Possible Topics

- Rating systems on CDs, video games, and movies
- Violence on the news and violence in movies
- Parental control over children's TV viewing/video game playing
- Censoring violent acts in movies (blacking out images, "blipping" out language, etc.)
- Government control of TV

Questions

1. _____

    _____

2. _____

    _____

3. _____

    _____

Expressing Your Opinion, Agreeing, and Disagreeing

You can use the following expressions to state your opinion.

Expressing Opinion

I think . . .
In my opinion . . .
As far as I'm concerned . . .
I'd rather . . .
If it were up to me . . .
The way I see it . . .
I'd prefer . . .
The reason why is . . .

Agreeing and Disagreeing Quickly

Look back at Chapter 1 to review expressions of agreement and disagreement. Also consider the following short responses of agreement and disagreement to show your classmates that you are listening to their opinions.

If you agree with someone who is making an affirmative statement using "I," you can agree by saying "Me too."

A: I think the government should control video game sales.
B: Me too.

If you agree with someone making a negative statement using "I," you can reply with something negative such as "neither" or "either."

A: I don't think the government should control video game sales.
B: Me neither or I don't either.

To disagree with a negative statement, you need to use contrastive stress with the auxiliary verb. In addition, you should add something to avoid miscommunication.

A: Video games don't desensitize teenagers to violence.
B: Yes, they DO (desensitize teenagers).*

*If you simply said, "Yes" without the additional information, your listeners would be confused.

ACTIVITY 20 **Discussing questions in small groups**

Your instructor will distribute one set of discussion questions from all the groups that submitted them. On the chart that follows, write down the opinions and reasons your group members provide.

Topic: _____

Classmate	Opinion	Reasons
	Support Oppose	
	Support Oppose	
	Support Oppose	
	Support Oppose	

ACTIVITY 21 **Summarizing opinions of group discussions**

Each group's reporter can share the information from his/her group with the whole class or your instructor may form new groups including at least one member from the first groups. Share your information from your chart.

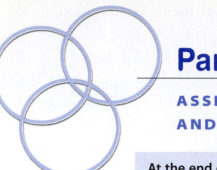

Part 3

ASSESSING YOUR LISTENING AND SPEAKING SKILLS

At the end of each chapter, you will find some tasks that will help you and your instructor evaluate whether you have learned the skills presented in the chapter. In addition, you will find some activities that ask you to reflect on your own progress.

ACTIVITY 22 Using contrastive stress

Work with a partner. Take turns reading the statements that follow but change one word to make the statement incorrect. Your partner will respond to you by "correcting" the statement using the information below.

Example:

Eighty percent of Americans believe television violence is harmful to society.*

Student A: Seventy percent of Americans believe television violence is harmful to society.

Student B: That's not true, it's EIGHTY percent.

Student A: Eighty percent of Koreans believe television violence is harmful to society.

Student B: No, it's 80 percent of AMERICANS who believe violence is harmful to society.

1. Fourth grade girls (59 percent) and boys (73 percent) report that the majority of their favorite video games are violent.†

2. Forty percent of the violent acts committed by "bad" characters were not punished.‡

---

* Source: *American Public Opinion on Media Violence.* 2000. Issue Briefs. Studio City, Calif.: Mediascope Press.
† Source: *The Impact of Violent Video Games* by Dr. Craig A. Anderson, Iowa State University, October 22, 2001.
‡ Source: *The Impact of Violent Television Programs and Movies*, by Dr. Brad J. Bushman, Iowa State University, October 8, 2001.

3. Most kids aren't aware of the messages contained in the lyrics to their favorite songs.*

4. By the time a child is eighteen, he or she will have watched 200,000 acts of violence including 40,000 murders on television.†

ACTIVITY 23 **Part 1:** **Applying the information**

Watch about a half hour of an action movie.‡ Use the chart that follows and keep track of the occurrences of each act of violence during the hour (make a ✓ in the box every time you see one of these violent acts).

Movie Title: _____

Act of violence	# of incidences
Shouting at someone or something	
Hitting someone or something	
Shooting someone or something	
Recklessly driving a car	
Crashing a car into something/someone	
Other:	

*Source: American Academy of Pediatrics: Impact of Music Lyrics and Music Videos on Children and Youth, 1996.

†Source: Huston, A.C. et al (1992). *Big world, small screen: The role of television in American society.* Lincoln, NE: University of Nebraska Press.

‡Adapted activity from "The Violence Formula: Analyzing TV, Video, and Movies" by Barbara Osborn, from www.medialit.org/reading_room/article94.html. Reprinted by permission of the Center for Media Literacy.

Part 2: Applying the information: discussing with a group

Assign members of your group the roles you learned in Chapter 1: leader, reporter, and participant(s). Explain briefly the movies that each of you watched, and discuss the following questions.

1. In your opinion, do you think the movie you watched was overly violent? Why or why not?

2. Do you think the violence played an important role in the story of the movie? How?

3. Do you think the movie would have been OK without the violence?

4. Were any consequences of the violence shown?

5. Did you see people hurt or bleeding?

6. Did any characters die? Did you see what happened to them?

7. How did the movie portray the good guys and the bad guys? What kinds of violence did the good guys use? The bad guys? Why did they use it? Were there any differences between the good guys and bad guys in their use of violence?

ACTIVITY 24 **Assessing participation in group work**

Your instructor may use this checklist to assess your participation in group work and use of academic English.

Group discussion	OK	Needs work	Example(s)
Preparation:			
• participates in a constructive manner			
• encourages others to participate			
Strategies:			
• is an active listener			
• disagrees in an agreeable manner			
• supports his/her opinions using facts, examples, statistics, or personal experiences			
Strategies:			
• uses syllable stress appropriately on academic words			
• uses contrastive stress when appropriate			

STRATEGY

Supporting Opinions

In both writing and discussions, it is important that you support your statements using a variety of techniques. You can support your opinions by doing one or more of the following:

Your opinion plus one of the following . . .

A *fact* to show that your opinion is based on something true, not just on your personal feelings

An *example* to describe a situation, either hypothetical or real, to support your opinion

A *statistic* from research to provide observable, measurable numbers to support your opinion

A *personal story* from your own experience—or someone else's— to support your opinion

= a supported opinion!

Master Student Tip

In academic courses, it is important to support your opinions with information from reputable sources.

ACTIVITY 25 **Synthesizing information in writing**

Use the information from this chapter, your lecture notes, and your class discussion notes to write a one-paragraph response to the following question.

Should the amount of violence on TV be regulated? Why or why not?

ACTIVITY 26 Evaluating your progress

Listed below are the objectives that were presented at the beginning of the chapter. Read through each one carefully, and evaluate your progress by checking: "Definitely need more help!", "Need a bit more practice!" or "Got it!"

Objectives	Definitely need more help!	Need a bit more practice!	Got it!
Learn word forms, syllable stress patterns, and meanings of academic words in context			
Recognize points of view in readings and lecture content			
Identify and use contrastive stress			
Use signal words of cause and effect to aid in note-taking			
Take lecture notes on a controversial topic			
Identify facts and opinions			
Demonstrate active listening and questioning skills in discussions			
Express opinions using academically appropriate language			
Use information from course material to support an opinion			

WEB POWER

You will find additional exercises related to the content in this chapter at **http://elt.thomson.com/collegeoral**.

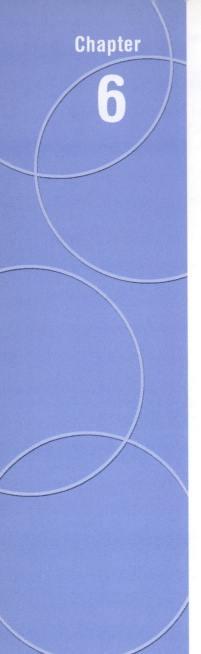

Are They Telling the Truth?

ACADEMIC FOCUS:
ETHICS ▶ PROFESSIONAL CODES

Academic Speaking and Listening Goals

In this chapter, you will continue to develop your skills as an academic listener and speaker. You will work individually, in pairs, and in small groups to:

- Identify syllable number, stress, and word forms in academic vocabulary
- Apply professional reading to lecture and discussion content
- Review a lecture's content using different strategies
- Ask clarification questions during class or instructor's office hours
- Use your notes for discussion and outside homework assignments
- Analyze case studies in discussion groups to apply lecture and reading content
- Use intonation for different types of questions
- Give a presentation to a partner about a case study

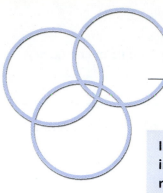

Part 1

EFFECTIVE ACADEMIC LISTENING

In this chapter, you will learn some of the language skills that are important in an ethics course, concentrating more specifically on the responsibilities of journalists and your responsibility as a media consumer. You will hear a lecture about how to be a smart news consumer by detecting bias in the news. As you learn about this topic, you will continue participating in listening, note-taking, and speaking activities.

○ Getting Ready for the Lecture

In addition to textbook material, college instructors may bring in outside reading from the profession in which she/he has worked or is working to provide you with additional authentic, accurate information. These readings often contain information your instructor can use to prepare you for lectures and discussions.

ACTIVITY 1 Identifying word forms and meanings

Choose the appropriate word form depending on its use in the sentence. Write the word's meaning using the context of the sentence.

1. The (*diversity / diverse*) international student population on the campus attracts students from all over the city.

   Meaning in context: _____

2. The teacher could (*perceive / perception / perceptive*) by the looks on her students' faces that they were nervous about the final exam.

   Meaning in context: _____

3. The student (*orient / orientation*) provided incoming freshmen with an opportunity to meet new people and walk around the campus.

   Meaning in context: _____

4. To get a quick (*response* / *respond*) from the police in an emergency, it's best to call 911.

Meaning in context: _____

5. I cannot (*justify* / *justification*) buying a new television at this time when my old one is working perfectly.

Meaning in context: _____

6. A student's (*motivated* / *motivation* / *motivate*) in a course usually depends on how much she/he likes the subject and the instructor.

Meaning in context: _____

7. If I (*pursuit* / *pursue*) a biology degree, I'll need to take at least seven courses in the science department.

Meaning in context: _____

8. For some people, cloning humans and other animals is (*ethical* / *ethically*) wrong.

Meaning in context: _____

9. Even though the man was found guilty in court yesterday, he continued to (*deny* / *denial* / *deniable*) that he had stolen $100,000 from Bridgeview Bank.

Meaning in context: _____

10. In order to receive $200 off the purchase of a new computer, you need to purchase it soon. The offer is only (*valid* / *validity*) through next week.

Meaning in context: _____

11. New medical research has been focusing on developing blood tests that can (*detection* / *detect*) whether a person carries certain forms of cancer.

Meaning in context: _____

12. It will probably not be (*feasible* / *feasibility*) for us to finish the project by tomorrow; one more week is necessary.

Meaning in context: _____

ACTIVITY 2 Learning the pronunciation of new words

Use the strategies you have learned in previous chapters to identify the syllables and stress of the following words from the reading and lecture.

1. diverse [___ - ___]

2. perceive [___ - ___]

3. ethical [___ - ___]

4. respond [___ - ___]

5. orientation [___ - ___]

6. bias [___ - ___]

7. validity [___ - ___]

8. ethnic [___ - ___]

9. denial [___ - ___]

10. pursuit [___ - ___]

11. detect [___ - ___]

12. justify [___ - ___]

13. motive [___ - ___]

14. feasible [___ - ___]

ACTIVITY 3   **Preparing for a reading's content**

To prepare for this chapter's content, you will be reading the Society of Professional Journalists Code of Ethics. Read the Society's four major principles* and then determine which standard of practice best matches each principle. Write the letter(s) in the space provided.

a. Seek Truth and Report It → Journalists should be honest, fair, and courageous in gathering, reporting, and interpreting information.

b. Minimize Harm → Ethical journalists treat sources, subjects, and colleagues as human beings deserving of respect.

c. Act Independently → Journalists should be free of obligation to any interest other than the public's right to know.

d. Be Accountable → Journalists are accountable to their readers, listeners, viewers, and each other.

1. _____ Never plagiarize.

2. _____ Expose unethical practices of journalists and the news media.

3. _____ Refuse gifts, favors, fees, free travel, and special treatment.

4. _____ Be sensitive when seeking or using interviews or photographs of those affected by tragedy or grief.

5. _____ Never distort the content of news photos or video.

6. _____ Identify sources whenever feasible. The public is entitled to as much information as possible on sources' reliability.

* Adapted: The Society of Professional Journalists Code of Ethics, https://www.spj.org/ethics_code.asp

ACTIVITY 4   **Reading to prepare for lecture and case studies**

Now read the complete Code of Ethics. Put a question mark (?) in the margins next to any standard of practice that you do not understand.

Society of Professional Journalists
Code of Ethics

Seek Truth and Report It

Journalists should:

- Test the accuracy of information from all sources and exercise care to avoid inadvertent error. Deliberate distortion is never permissible.
- Diligently seek out subjects of news stories to give them the opportunity to respond to allegations of wrongdoing.
- Identify sources whenever feasible. The public is entitled to as much information as possible on sources' reliability.
- Always question sources' motives before promising anonymity. Clarify conditions attached to any promise made in exchange for information. Keep promises.
- Make certain that headlines, news teases and promotional material, photos, video, audio, graphics, sound bites and quotations do not misrepresent. They should not oversimplify or highlight incidents out of context.
- Never distort the content of news photos or video. Image enhancement for technical clarity is always permissible. Label montages and photo illustrations.
- Avoid misleading re-enactments or staged news events. If re-enactment is necessary to tell a story, label it.
- Avoid undercover or other surreptitious methods of gathering information except when traditional open methods will not yield information vital to the public. Use of such methods should be explained as part of the story.

- Never plagiarize.
- Tell the story of the diversity and magnitude of the human experience boldly, even when it is unpopular to do so.
- Examine their own cultural values and avoid imposing those values on others.
- Avoid stereotyping by race, gender, age, religion, ethnicity, geography, sexual orientation, disability, physical appearance or social status.
- Support the open exchange of views, even views they find repugnant.
- Give voice to the voiceless; official and unofficial sources of information can be equally valid.
- Distinguish between advocacy and news reporting. Analysis and commentary should be labeled and not misrepresent fact or context.
- Distinguish news from advertising and shun hybrids that blur the lines between the two.
- Recognize a special obligation to ensure that the public's business is conducted in the open and that government records are open to inspection.

Minimize Harm

Journalists should:

- Show compassion for those who may be affected adversely by news coverage. Use special sensitivity when dealing with children and inexperienced sources or subjects.
- Be sensitive when seeking or using interviews or photographs of those affected by tragedy or grief.

- Recognize that gathering and reporting information may cause harm or discomfort. Pursuit of the news is not a license for arrogance.
- Recognize that private people have a greater right to control information about themselves than do public officials and others who seek power, influence or attention. Only an overriding public need can justify intrusion into anyone's privacy.
- Be cautious about identifying juvenile suspects or victims of sex crimes.
- Be judicious about naming criminal suspects before the formal filing of charges.
- Balance a criminal suspect's fair trial rights with the public's right to be informed.

Act Independently

Journalists should:

- Avoid conflicts of interest, real or perceived.
- Remain free of associations and activities that may compromise integrity or damage credibility.
- Refuse gifts, favors, fees, free travel and special treatment, and shun secondary employment, political involvement, public office and service in community organizations if they compromise journalistic integrity.

- Disclose unavoidable conflicts.
- Be vigilant and courageous about holding those with power accountable.
- Deny favored treatment to advertisers and special interests and resist their pressure to influence news coverage.
- Be wary of sources offering information for favors or money; avoid bidding for news.

Be Accountable

Journalists should:

- Clarify and explain news coverage and invite dialogue with the public over journalistic conduct.
- Encourage the public to voice grievances against the news media.
- Admit mistakes and correct them promptly.
- Expose unethical practices of journalists and the news media.
- Abide by the same high standards to which they hold others.

 **STRATEGY**

Asking Questions for Clarification

If you don't understand part of a reading or lecture, don't be afraid to ask the professor to clarify what you read or what (s)he said. Most of the time other students have the same or a similar question, so you will not only be helping yourself, but you will also help clarify the information for your classmates. Preparing questions for a visit to your instructor during her/his office hours is also a successful strategy. It's your responsibility as a student to make sure that you understand, and it's the instructor's responsibility to help you understand.

ACTIVITY 5 **Preparing clarification questions**

The "Society of Professional Journalists Code of Ethics" reading contains a lot of information. Choose four of the question marks (?) you made in the reading in Activity 4. Write four questions to ask your instructor during class or during her/his office hours. Make sure your questions are specific by describing the exact location in the reading.

Bad examples: What does the reading mean?

Why do we have to read this article?

What does "unavoidable conflict" mean?

Good examples: What's an example of an "unavoidable conflict" mentioned in the third principle, "Act Independently"?

What does "diligently" mean in the second standard of practice under "Seek Truth and Report It"?

What's an example of a "repugnant view" under "Seek Truth and Report It"?

1. _____

_____

2. _____

_____

3. _____

_____

4. _____

_____

ACTIVITY 6 **Getting information from your classmates**

Share your questions from Activity 5 with a small group of classmates and help each other answer the questions. Any remaining unanswered questions can be asked in a whole-class discussion or at an appointment during your instructor's office hours.

ACTIVITY **7** **Applying the information from the reading**

There have been many controversial situations over the years in which journalists, photographers, and editors have had to refer back to the Code of Ethics to make decisions. Read each of the situations below and discuss which principle(s) from the code are in question.

1. Jayson Blair resigned from the *New York Times* after he was accused of fake reporting and plagiarism. Blair wrote a front page story about the family of an Army soldier who was killed in action in Iraq. Blair quoted the soldier's mother and described their home, but the mother said she had never talked to Blair—on the phone or in person. In addition, an editor from a Texas newspaper claims Blair plagiarized the story from one of their reporters.
   a. Seek Truth and Report It
   b. Minimize Harm
   c. Act Independently
   d. Be Accountable

2. In 1986, even though a police officer tried to stop him, a news photographer took a photo of a five-year-old boy being zipped up in a body bag after he had drowned; grieving members of the boy's family were also in the photo.
   a. Seek Truth and Report It
   b. Minimize Harm
   c. Act Independently
   d. Be Accountable

3. In 1998, one columnist resigned from *The Boston Globe* after being accused of making up sources and stealing material from other reporters. Another columnist, two months earlier, was fired for making up characters and dialogue.
   a. Seek Truth and Report It
   b. Minimize Harm
   c. Act Independently
   d. Be Accountable

4. In 2003, two reporters from *The Salt Lake Tribune* were fired for selling rumors about the Elizabeth Smart case to the tabloid *National Enquirer* for $20,000.
   a. Seek Truth and Report It
   b. Minimize Harm
   c. Act Independently
   d. Be Accountable

○ Getting Information from An Instructor's Lecture

The lecture you will hear is about different types of bias that you may encounter when reading, watching, and/or listening to the news.

ACTIVITY **8**   **Part 1:** **Understanding the power of opinion**

Briefly look at this photo and then close your book. On a separate sheet of paper, write what you think is happening in the photo.

Part 2: **Understanding the influence of opinion and point of view**

Take turns describing what you wrote in Part 1 to your partner. Discuss the reasons for the similarities or the differences.

STRATEGY

Using an Instructor's Guide Notes

Some instructors may use PowerPoint or pass out an outline to present lectures. Even though these materials provide effective visual clues and organization, it is essential that you still take notes, directly on the handout if possible. Why? The instructor doesn't always provide *all* the information; you must add the details and examples.

ACTIVITY 9 **Identifying types of bias**

The lecture you are going to hear is about how to detect different types of bias in the news. With a partner, discuss how these situations are not objective and how they may relate to the Code of Ethics in Activity 4.

1. One newspaper publishes photographs of two presidential candidates on the front page; however, one photo is on the top half of the paper—"above the fold"—and the other is on the bottom half—"below the fold."

2. News media refer to women whose husbands have died as "widows" but hardly ever refer to men whose wives have died as "widowers."

3. A headline on the front page of a local newspaper reads "School Budget Increased 5%". However, the full story explains that for the past seven years, the budget has increased 5 percent each year.

4. One radio talk show host talks about "affirmative action" programs, while a different host calls them "racial preference" programs.

5. One cable channel devotes ten minutes of its morning news program to a story about a CEO's resignation from a large company; a different cable channel has a thirty-second report of the resignation.

 ACTIVITY 10 **Adding information to instructor's handout**

Now you will listen to a lecture and take notes directly on a handout to help you prepare to discuss case studies. An example of including additional information is given in the introduction.

How to Detect Bias in the News

• Introduction: Bias in the News
    ■ Journalists try to be objective → Interviewer, writer/s, photographer, editor/s
    ■ All news stories are influenced
    ■ Most bias ≠ deliberate
    ■ Several techniques that may "creep in"

- Bias through placement
  - First-page stories more significant than those in the back (local and national papers may differ)
  - Stories at the beginning of TV and radio programs are more significant

- Bias by headline
  - Reading headlines only
  - Importance of paper fold
  - Potential for misleading headlines

- Bias through photos, captions, and camera angles
  - Flattering vs. bad photos
  - Camera angles

- Bias through names and titles
  - Use of labels
  - Potential influence

- Bias through statistics and crowd counts
  - Inflating or deflating numbers

- Word Choice and Tone
  - Positive and negative words

Excerpted from Newskit: A Consumers Guide to News Media by Jeffrey Schrank, The Learning Seed Co. Used by permission of the author.

⭕ Making Your Notes Useful

ACTIVITY 11 **Reviewing the lecture's content**

With a partner, use one of the strategies below to review your notes:

- Ask each other clarification questions to fill in missing content.
- Take turns summarizing the different types of biases.
- Predict a list of short answer test questions.

ACTIVITY 12 Identifying types of bias

Go back to Activity 9 and identify which type(s) of bias each situation demonstrates based on what you heard in the lecture.

ACTIVITY 13 Using your notes to find examples of bias

Using your lecture notes, find three examples of the types of bias described in the lecture in print or online newspapers. Indicate the type(s) of bias used and describe it (or bring in actual examples).

Type of bias (see lecture notes)	Description
Headline, word choice: "Gov't Spending Against Terrorism Too Low"	The choice of the word "too" makes it seem like more money should be spent on fighting terrorism. The word "too" shows bias.
Photo of a large group of people at a demonstration in the park	The photo makes it look like there were more people than there really were. The caption mentions that twenty people were there; it looks like more.

Part 2

EFFECTIVE ACADEMIC SPEAKING

STRATEGY

Using Different Types of Question Intonation in Group Discussions

A very important aspect of pronunciation is intonation. Intonation, or a change in pitch, is what we hear when someone's voice goes up or down. This intonation can easily change the meaning of a statement or question. In other words, *how* you say something is sometimes more important than *what* you say. Different types of questions have different intonation patterns.

Information Questions (who, what, where, when, why, and how)—the pitch goes down

What is your opinion on the topic?

Yes/No Questions (do/does, is/are, was/were, etc.)—the pitch goes up

Do you think the photo should be published?

Tag Questions—the pitch goes down for the statement and then up

She's a politician, isn't she?
He should not take a photo, should he?
You don't think she's guilty, do you?

Tag questions can be a good way to express your opinion, to seek agreement from others, to disagree with someone politely, and to involve more people in a discussion.

ACTIVITY 14   Using question intonation

Complete the following questions from a group discussion with a tag question. Practice saying these questions out loud using correct intonation.

1. Privacy is more important than the public's right to know,

_____?

2. The editors are responsible for printing the truth,

_____?

3. You don't think that movie stars have the right to total privacy,

_____?

4. Television cameras should not be allowed in courtrooms,

_____?

5. The paparazzi shouldn't be allowed at funerals,

_____?

STRATEGY

Developing Critical Thinking Skills by Analyzing Case Studies

Case studies are examples of real-life situations in which ideas from a course can be discussed. In an ethics course, students might be asked to read particular cases and discuss what they would do if they were in the situation. In their discussion, students would be expected to use information from lectures and readings as well as strategies for expressing opinion, agreement, and disagreement.

Discussing case studies helps students to:

- develop critical thinking skills
- improve organizational skills
- enhance communication skills
- work collaboratively with others

ACTIVITY 15   **Part 1:** **Analyzing case studies**

In the next activity, your group will act as newspaper editors. Review the reading in Activity 4 and discuss the following questions in a whole-class discussion.

1. In your opinion(s), what is the role of a newspaper editor?
2. Is it always necessary for the editor and newspaper journalists to tell the whole truth? Why or why not?
3. Very often, the public's right to know the truth and the right to privacy are in conflict with each other. In what situations do you think one is more important than the other and vice versa? Why?

Part 2: **Analyzing case studies**

Your instructor will assign each group one of the following situations. These are situations from the London Free Press,* *and the* Chicago Sun-Times.† *There are no right or wrong answers to the questions, but instructors expect your discussion to be based on information presented in assigned readings and the lectures. Follows these directions:*

- *Assign group members the following roles (refer to Chapter 1): leader, reporter, and participant(s).*
- *Discuss the case study and reach a unanimous decision (use the reading and lecture notes from this chapter).*
- *Present the decision to the whole class (reporter).*[1]

Case A

It is your newspaper's policy to include cause of death whenever possible in obituaries of newsworthy people. A prominent cleric dies but relatives refuse to discuss cause of death. A reporter is able to confirm from a close family member the cause was an AIDS-related illness. Do you go against the wishes of the family and print that AIDS was the cause of death OR list the cause as complications of pneumonia, without reference to AIDS? Why?

---

*Source: Selected Case Studies #2, "Editorial POVs," and #5, "Story," (slightly adapted to include questions), London (Ontario) Free Press. Reprinted by permission.

†Source: Selected Case Studies #1 and #9, (slightly adapted to include questions) from the "You Were the Editor" by Gary Wisby, *Chicago Sun-Times*, Sunday, July 23, 2000. Reprinted with special permission from the Chicago Sun-Times, Inc., © 2004 and 2000.

---

1. Your instructor may share the results of this same activity done in the two newspapers.

Case B

A reporter and photographer are assigned to interview a popular politician who has recently completed an alcohol-recovery program paid for by a group of citizens. He is now pledged to a life of sobriety. One photo taken in his office reveals what appears to be a liquor bottle partially hidden in a bookcase, behind some folders. Do you erase the bottle from the picture OR publish the picture intact and let readers come to their own conclusions? Why?

Case C

Your reporter discovers that police know a particular neighborhood is being stalked by a rapist. They haven't publicized the information because they think they are closing in on the suspect. The police ask your newspaper not to publish the story, fearing it will tip off the suspected rapist to the investigation. Hold off on the story in hopes the police will catch the man, some editors say. Others argue women in the neighborhood should be warned. Do you print the story? Why or why not?

Case D

A leading female federal official heads the battle to outlaw abortion. She is a regular at anti-abortion rallies. Your reporter finds out that the politician recently accompanied her married daughter to an abortion clinic where the daughter had an abortion. Some of your editors say the story invades the daughter's privacy and shouldn't be printed. Others say it shows clear deceit on the politician's part, and the public should know. Do you print the story? Why or why not?

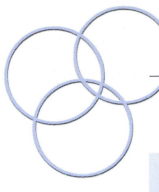

Part 3

ASSESSING YOUR LISTENING AND SPEAKING SKILLS

At the end of each chapter, you will find some tasks that will help you and your instructor evaluate whether you have learned the skills presented in the chapter. In addition, you will find some activities that ask you to reflect on your own progress.

ACTIVITY 16 Analyzing a case study with a partner

Sit with a partner. One of you will be assigned Case A and the other will be assigned Case B. Discuss how you would deal with the situation if you were the photo editor.

Case A

Each month, photographers all over the world submit their best photos to various photographers' organizations and associations. A photo similar to the one below won a first place. Here, a Bosnian woman grieves at the grave of one of her two sons killed defending Bosnia.

If you were the editor of the newspaper, would you have published this photo? Why or why not? Under what circumstances?

Case B

The July 2003 issue of *Redbook* has a photo of Julia Roberts on the cover. The photo is a combination of two different photos taken at two different times. Magazines sometimes do this when a star refuses or is unable to take time for a cover photo session. On this cover, the head of Julia Roberts is a photo from the 2002 People's Choice Awards and the body is from the 1999 premiere of the movie *Notting Hill*. Julia Roberts did not give her permission to blend the photos.

Redbook is not a news magazine. Its target audience is women. Many articles relate to health and beauty. Do you think it's okay for a magazine to use a photo that is a combination of two different photos? Why or why not?

○ Assessing Presentations of Case Studies to a Partner

Your instructor may use this checklist to assess your participation in
Activity 16.

Pair presentation	OK	Needs work	Example(s)
Preparation:			
• accurately presented the issue			
• provided opinion supported with information from reading and lecture			
Strategies:			
• expressed opinions effectively			
• uses syllable stress appropriately on academic words			
• uses contrastive stress, intonation, etc. when appropriate			

ACTIVITY 17 **Part 1:** **Adding notes to the syllabus description**

Listen to your instructor describe a semester project as you read the section of the syllabus. Add important information to the syllabus excerpt that follows. Ask clarification questions if appropriate.

Fall Semester Project

Assignment: Four Position Papers

Purpose: to answer four different ethical questions defending your point of view on a question.

Criteria:
- Completed outside of class
- Based on ethical conflict questions listed on syllabus
  - Topics limited to two questions per due date (e.g. questions 1 or 2 for the first paper, 3 or 4 for the second paper, etc.)
- Two page minimum
- 20-point scale (20 points = A); 5 points for spelling and grammar

Due Dates:
- Position paper #1 DUE January 21
- Position paper #2 DUE February 5
- Position paper #3 DUE March 5
- Position paper #4 DUE April 23

Alternative: classroom presentation

Criteria:
- Topic of your choice
- Sign up required*
- 10 minutes/Q & A

*signing up requires you to complete the presentation on the specified date; if not, you will receive an "F"

Part 2: Adding notes to the syllabus description of a project

Answer the following questions based on the description you heard and your notes.

1. Do the position papers have to be typed?

2. In addition to the position papers being due on January 21, February 5, and March 5, what else will take place during class on those days?

3. What is the last day of class?

4. How many topic choices do you have for each position paper?

5. Can you choose question #4 for the first position paper?

6. What happens if you sign up for a presentation for a certain date but do not complete it?

7. Can you do two presentations in place of two position papers?

8. Would you choose to do a presentation in place of a paper? Why or why not?

ACTIVITY 18 **Evaluating your progress**

Listed below are the objectives that were presented at the beginning of the chapter. Read through each one carefully, and evaluate your progress by checking: "Definitely need more help!", "Need a bit more practice!" or "Got it!"

Objectives	Definitely need more help!	Need a bit more practice!	Got it!
Identify syllable number, stress, and word forms in academic vocabulary			
Apply professional reading to lecture and discussion content			
Review a lecture's content using different strategies			
Ask clarification questions during class or instructor's office hours			
Use your notes for discussion and outside homework assignments			
Analyze case studies in discussion groups to apply lecture and reading content			
Use intonation for different types of questions			
Give a presentation to a partner about a case study			

WEB POWER

You will find additional exercises related to the content in this chapter at http://elt.thomson.com/collegeoral.